Mastering English through Global Debate

**Mastering Languages
through Global Debate**

Mastering **English**
through Global Debate

Ekaterina Talalakina

Tony Brown

Jennifer Bown

William Eggington

Georgetown University Press | Washington, DC

Library of Congress Cataloging-in-Publication Data

Talalakina, Ekaterina.
    Mastering English through global debate/Ekaterina Talalakina, Tony Brown, Jennifer Bown, and William Eggington.
        pages cm.
    Includes bibliographical references and index.
    ISBN 978-1-62616-081-1 (pbk. : alk. paper)
    1. English language—Study and teaching—Foreign speakers. 2. English language—Conversation and phrase books.   I. Title.
    PE1128.A2T24 2014
    428.2'4—dc23
                                                                2014013577

∞ This book is printed on acid-free paper meeting the requirements of the American National Standard for Permanence in Paper for Printed Library Materials.

21 20 19 18 17 16 15 14   9 8 7 6 5 4 3 2   First printing

Text design by click! Publishing Services
Cover design by Martha Madrid Design Studio
Cover image © Igor E./Image Source/Corbis

To aspiring foreign language learners throughout the world
in pursuit of truth through reasoned debate.

CONTENTS

Units

FOREWORD

Mastering English through Global Debate brings together the strong rhetorical traditions of the communication field and the best practices of adult second-language instruction within a new form of an advanced, foreign language textbook. Whereas debate textbooks exist in ESL literature, the debate tradition is largely absent from the foreign language textbook literature. Advanced- and Superior-level tasks, as represented in the corresponding level descriptions of the American Council on the Teaching of Foreign Languages (ACTFL), align well with the debate, as speech genre, specifically: supporting opinion, discussing an abstract topic, hypothesizing, tailoring language, persuading, advocating a position at length, and using sophisticated verbal strategies.

Language specialists increasingly recognize the value of debate as a means of facilitating advanced-level foreign language uptake and overall discourse development. This textbook provides level-specific scaffolding activities that prepare students step by step to participate fully in debates with their classmates. The textbook affords students authentic communicative experiences within academically relevant content areas, which motivate students and position them to succeed in a range of advanced-level speech situations, both interpersonal and presentational. *Mastering English through Global Debate* is intended to help learners improve their English speaking skills, even as they learn to read and think critically, write persuasively, and construct sound oral arguments for formal presentations in the target language.

Dan E. Davidson
President, American Councils for International Education

ACKNOWLEDGMENTS

The authors are greatly indebted to Sharon Tavares for providing invaluable input in the form of both materials development and technical expertise as a formatting editor. Thanks also go to Kristy Stewart and members of the Faculty Editing Services at Brigham Young University (BYU), who played a critical role in the final stages of format editing.

We would like to thank the editorial staff at Georgetown University Press for their insightful feedback and attention to detail. In particular, we are indebted to David Nicholls, acquisitions editor; Deborah Weiner, former editorial and production manager; and Glenn Saltzman, editorial, design, and production manager.

The authors also wish to thank colleagues at Brigham Young University, in particular, John Rosenberg of the College of Humanities and Ray Clifford of the Center for Language Studies, for supporting this project from its infancy as a research proposal through to its publication as a textbook.

In addition, special thanks go to Irina Yakusheva, Chair of the Department of Foreign Languages at the National Research University Higher School of Economics (NRU HSE), Moscow, Russia, for field-testing materials in English as a Foreign Language (EFL) classrooms. We also wish to thank administrators at NRU HSE for supporting innovations in language education, including videoconferencing technology that made connecting students from BYU and NRU HSE possible. Members of the technical support team at NRU HSE facilitated videoconference debates.

On the BYU side, videoconference debates were made possible thanks to Mel Smith of the Humanities Technology and Research Support Center. Harold Hendricks of the BYU Humanities Learning Resources provided a state-of-the-art recording studio and sound engineering equipment, and Nicholas Lambson recorded and edited each of the audio recordings. Spencer Carter, Julia Carter, Joseph Skousen, and Jessica Spencer are featured in the mock debate audio recordings and Melinda Semadeni and Brandtley Henderson in the chapter texts.

Additionally, we wish to thank Grant Newman, Brooke Ward, Michelle Jeffs, and Stanley Lloyd for extensive materials development of chapter texts and sample position papers.

INTRODUCTION

Mastering English through Global Debate is designed for students who have attained Advanced-level proficiency according to the guidelines established by the American Council on the Teaching of Foreign Languages. As such, the textbook's primary objective is to facilitate acquisition of Superior-level proficiency.

In order to progress from Advanced- to Superior-level proficiency, learners must be able to discuss abstract topics, express and support opinions, hypothesize, and tailor their language to specific audiences. Debate offers a powerful forum for developing and honing this skill set. The topics selected for *Mastering English through Global Debate* are environment versus economy, interventionism versus isolationism, wealth redistribution versus self-reliance, cultural preservation versus diversity, security versus freedom, and education versus field experience. These pertinent topics will likely be of interest to adult language learners.

The Textbook's Structure

Mastering English through Global Debate contains six chapters, each of which begins with scaffolding exercises to introduce the topic to learners and activate their background knowledge. These exercises allow students to write and articulate their own ideas on each of the topics and prepare them for reading the texts that comprise the heart of each chapter.

At the center of each chapter is a text written by a native speaker of English. These texts are not simplified in any way and thus provide a rich source of input, particularly in terms of contextualized vocabulary. Each article presents an overview of the topics, including the major arguments on both sides of the debate, and each reading assignment is followed by comprehension checks.

A major portion of each chapter is dedicated to vocabulary development. Lexical items are introduced not as single words but rather as collocations—groups of words commonly used together. The vocabulary chosen for each chapter was, in part, governed by frequency of use as found in linguistic corpora. Students often are directed to use online corpora to further their word knowledge so that they learn words as they are used in the language, not in isolation. Open-ended discussion questions offer a starting point for learners to apply new vocabulary introduced in the articles.

Once students become acquainted with a topic and the vocabulary necessary for discussion, they turn their attention to preparing for the debate. In the "Constructing Critical Discourse" section, learners are introduced to advanced syntactical features of the language, particularly those used to form hypotheses—a function particularly important for performing at the Superior level. Students put their new knowledge to use in a role-play by representing various stakeholders discussing the issue in a concrete way.

In the "Listening" section, learners listen to brief mock debates that illustrate important turns of phrases used for turn-taking, arguing a point, agreeing, and disagreeing.

The final two sections, "Formatting the Argument: Writing" and "Formatting the Argument: Speaking," are the culminating tasks for the textbook, for which all of the other sections have been preparation. In the speaking section, learners are introduced to important rhetorical strategies used in debate, such as conjecture, questions of definition, and questions of value. In the writing portion, learners are introduced to the elements of persuasive writing, from writing a thesis statement to constructing paragraphs, and to strategies for revision. At the end of each section, learners put their skills to the test as they debate with other class members and write a persuasive essay, arguing one side of the issue.

This text can be used as a complete course or in conjunction with other materials.

NOTE ON WEB RESOURCES

In addition to *Mastering English through Global Debate,* students will have at their disposal the audio companion. The audio companion includes two recordings for each chapter—one reciting the feature article from the chapter and another giving a mock debate. Transcripts of the mock debates and directions are included in the audio companion. An icon in the text ▢ indicates whenever students should refer to an audio recording. The audio companion can be found and accessed for free in the Teacher's Resources section of the Georgetown University Press website, press.georgetown.edu/georgetown/instructors _manuals.

In this volume you will also find an icon ◉ directing you to consult the Corpus of Contemporary American English (COCA) website, http://corpus.byu.edu/coca/, which Brigham Young University provides as a public service. COCA is arguably the most widely used corpus of American English today. It is composed of 450 million words from 160,000 texts, including 20 million words each year from 1990 to the present. Structurally, it is evenly divided between the five genres of spoken discourse, fiction, magazines, newspapers, and academic journals. Moreover, it allows users to carry out in-depth research on a wide range of lexical, phraseological, morphological, syntactic, and semantic phenomena in English.

Instructors will be interested in the supplemental answer key. It is available in the Teacher's Resources section of the Georgetown University Press website, press.georgetown .edu/georgetown/instructors_manuals. Finally, we refer instructors to the digital short by Tony Brown and Jennifer Bown, *Teaching Advanced Language Skills through Global Debate: Theory and Practice*, which is available for purchase from Georgetown University Press and other ebook vendors.

ABBREVIATIONS AND ACRONYMS

ACTFL	American Council on the Teaching of Foreign Languages
CD	compact disc
CEO	chief executive officer
COCA	Corpus of Contemporary American English
CTF	Combined Task Force
DREAM	Development Relief and Education for Alien Minors
DC	District of Columbia
e.g.	for example
EPA	Environmental Protection Agency
EPI	Economic Policy Institute
etc.	et cetera (and so forth)
EU	European Union
ex.	example
GDP	gross domestic product
G.I.	government issue
GWOT	global war on terror
HR	human resources
IT	information technology
OECD	Organization for Economic Co-operation and Development
PATRIOT	Providing Appropriate Tools Required to Intercept and Obstruct Terrorism
PhD	doctor of philosophy
St.	saint
syn.	synonym
UNESCO	United Nations Educational, Scientific and Cultural Organization
US	United States
v.	versus
vs.	versus
WEF	World Economic Forum

UNIT
1

Environment versus Economy

Global Priorities: Being Green or Earning Green

Pre-Reading

Introducing the Issue

A. With a partner discuss the following questions using the photographs and corresponding descriptions.

1. What do you know about each of these events? Where/when did they take place?
2. Do you think these catastrophes are natural or man-made? Defend your answer by determining the root cause of each problem.
3. Do you have similar issues in your country? Tell your partner about environmental issues common in your country.

Oil spill kills or injures more than eight thousand animals.

Polar bears threatened by global warming.

Hundreds of flights canceled due to heavy smog. (Credit: "Beijing Smog" by Kevin Dooley, Chandler, AZ, US)

An explosion in a nuclear plant scatters radioactive debris. (Credit: By Digital Globe)

B. Study **Language Note 1** on the meanings of the word "green" presented through examples and synonyms (provided by *Oxford American Dictionary and Thesaurus*) and paraphrase the title "Global Priorities: Being Green or Earning Green" by substituting the word "green" with synonyms.

Language Note 1	
Green (ADJECTIVE)	**Green (NOUN)**
1. "a green scarf" Syn.: lime, olive, jade 2. "a green island" Syn.: grassy, leafy 3. "green issues" Syn.: environmental, ecological 4. "a green alternative" Syn.: nonpolluting, environmentally friendly 5. "green bananas" Syn.: unripe 6. "green lieutenant" Syn.: inexperienced, naïve 7. "green face" Syn.: pale, sick	1. "green on the road" Syn.: plants 2. "to eat greens" Syn.: vegetables 3. "Greens against corporations" Syn.: ecoactivists 4. "to save some green" (informal, dated) Syn.: money

C. In your own words, try to explain the title of the article "Global Priorities: Being Green or Earning Green."

D. Based on the title "Global Priorities: Being Green or Earning Green," make a list of issues that might appear in the article.

1. pollution
2. generating profit
3. _____
4. _____
5. _____
6. _____

Creating Mind Maps

A. Brainstorm as many words as you know associated with the challenges a country might face regarding the environment and the economy. Arrange your ideas to create two separate mind maps according to the pattern shown below. After reading the article, you will be able to add more information, so leaving boxes blank at this point is okay.

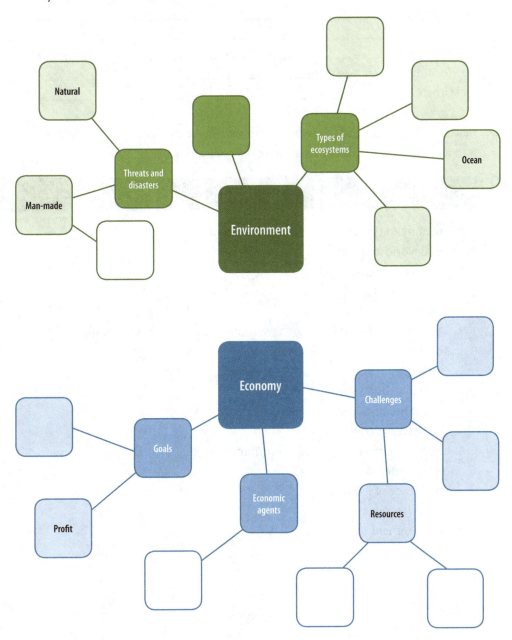

B. Compare your maps with those of your classmates to generate additional ideas. After completing each of the two maps, decide which topic areas can help bridge the gap between the two maps. In other words, which issues concerning environment and economy intersect?

C. Insert the words *environment*, *ecology*, *economy*, or *economics* in the blanks below to create collocations. Add appropriate articles when needed.
   1. A healthy _____
   2. To pollute _____
   3. Free-market _____
   4. To stimulate _____
   5. Urban _____

D. Match each derivative of the words *environment*, *ecology*, and *economy* with its definition and the words with which it can make collocations.

Definitions	Words	Collocates
1. relating to the natural world and the impact of human activity on its condition	a. environmental	A. product
2. not harmful to the environment	b. environmentally friendly	B. solution
3. giving good value or return in relation to the money, time, or effort expended	c. ecological	C. disaster
4. being characterized by the interdependence of living organisms in an environment	d. economical	D. protection

Discussing Facts and Opinions

Cultural Note 1   The two major political parties in the United States are known to have different views on a whole spectrum of issues, including the trade-off between environmental conservation and economic development. Democrats often place a higher importance on environmental conservation than economic development, and vice versa for Republicans.

A. Read the statements below and determine whether they represent the views of those in favor of Republicans or Democrats. Explain your answer to a partner.

    1. Economic prosperity is essential to environmental progress.

    2. It is our responsibility to protect America's extraordinary natural resources.

    3. People who own land also should protect it.

    4. The health of our families and the strength of our economy depend on our protection of the environment.

    5. We fight to strengthen laws that ensure we have clean air and water.

    6. We reject the false choice between a healthy economy and a healthy environment.

B. In your opinion, which of the six statements above reflect the dominant views of individuals in your country regarding the environment and economy? Explain.

Studying the Topic

Focused Reading

A. As you read "Global Priorities: Being Green or Earning Green," list the arguments for various sides of the debate (Environmentalists, Realists, and Skeptics) in the following table.

Environmentalists	Realists	Skeptics
•	•	•
•	•	•
•	•	•
•	•	•
•	•	•
•	•	•
•	•	•
•	•	•
•	•	•
•	•	•

B. Check your pronunciation of unfamiliar words from the text as you listen to Audio Recording 1.1.

Global Priorities: Being Green or Earning Green

Brooke Ward

Deep in the rainforests of Brazil, illegal logging creates space for economic opportunities. Ranchers needing to graze their cattle, farmers looking to bank on the profitable commercial soy bean industry, and opportunists hoping to cash in on the lucrative hardwood export market all jostle to control the vast tracts of land necessary to produce their fortunes. Despite conservation measures, even the Brazilian government has gotten involved by cutting into the Amazon with dams, power lines, roads, and oil and gas pipelines, all in the name of economic growth.[1]

As one of the fastest-growing major economies in the world, Brazil has benefited from a growth-centric focus, but at a cost, some say. The ensuing debate presents an interesting dilemma: should environmental considerations take precedence even when they're detrimental to the economy, or should the environment take a backseat to economic growth?

There are many who would suggest that the environment and the economy are not mutually exclusive. When campaigning for office, former US president Bill Clinton maintained that it was not necessary to sacrifice one for the other. "The choice between jobs and environment is a false one; you can have both."[2] Unfortunately, as many activists and policy- and lawmakers know, balancing the two priorities is easier said than done. Putting the environment first is seen as a luxury that few can afford, even in the mature economies of Europe and North America.

For those pegged as environmentalists, or those who would argue that environmental concerns should take first priority, the prevailing sentiment is that "we do not inherit the earth from our ancestors, we borrow it from our children."[3] Their belief is that we, as the human race, are at the peak of cultural and technological growth. Nonrenewable resources are overused, and eventually we will surpass the planet's capacity to sustain human life. If we don't make decisions to protect our resources and prevent pollution now, in time our progeny will not have clean air to breathe, safe water to drink, fertile soil in which to grow food, and so on. To paraphrase a Cree Indian proverb, it is only then that we will realize that we cannot eat money.

Environmentalists also point out that while running out of resources is projected for a far-off future, human safety and ability to thrive is already threatened in many areas. Safe drinking water is something that is taken for granted in North America, but there are recorded instances in Wyoming and the Canadian province of Alberta where residents could light their tap water on fire due to methane leeching into the water supply from nearby mining activities.[4]

Some of the most devastating impacts of human interaction on the environment are observed in developing nations and frequently are caused by large companies based in highly developed countries. They take advantage of developing nations' inability to exploit their own natural resources, often operate in areas of rampant corruption and lax regulation, and damage natural food sources that sustain local populations. For example, the multinational oil and gas company Royal Dutch Shell has operated in the Niger Delta for decades and, in its own words, "generate[s] billions of dollars of income for the government, create[s] jobs and provide[s] energy for the country . . . and spend[s] millions of dollars a year on community development."[5] Nevertheless, the region in which it operates remains plagued by poverty and violence because the government that Shell supports is corrupt and oppressive. Frequent oil spills also wreak havoc on surrounding water systems by damaging important fish breeding grounds and making the surviving fish, the protein staple for many communities, unsuitable for human consumption.[6]

The Brazilian rainforest illuminates the argument that nature has "ecosystem capital," an incalculable market value that often surpasses other economic activities that might happen within a given ecosystem.[7] The Amazon has a staggering array of unique plant and animal species from which we derive important medicines, pharmaceuticals, fibers, dyes, and so on. The forest is also known for water cycling (producing its own rain through moisture it releases into the atmosphere) and carbon sequestering (absorbing carbon dioxide from the atmosphere). In a normal year, for instance, the forest's carbon sink absorbs almost two billion tons of carbon dioxide, or close to 7 percent of the global population's annual emissions. However, almost 20 percent of the rainforest has been cut down in the last forty years alone.[8] This deforestation creates a dangerous downward spiral that includes desiccation, drought, pollution, soil erosion, and loss of biodiversity, all of which degrade quality of life for humans.

Anthropologists have theorized that the misuse and abuse of resources has played a significant role in the toppling of several ancient societies. As a foreboding microcosm of planet Earth, environmentalists sometimes point to Easter Island, the remote Chilean isle whose population dwindled to near extinction after rendering the isolated island treeless.[9] Ultimately, conservationists say that the environment is not merely a pressing issue; it is the lens through which mankind needs to see and approach all other issues, particularly economic growth.

On the other side of the coin are those who advocate for the economy as society's preeminent concern. This group can be divided into two main factions: realists, who feel that the state of the economy is a more pressing threat than the environment, and skeptics, who are generally opposed to the environmental movement as a whole. Realists argue that the economy is a more imminent threat because the effects of joblessness and poverty and the resulting social ramifications (hunger, violence, etc.) are evident now.

Sustained economic growth raises people out of poverty and improves the quality of life for today's global citizens in visible ways, including employment opportunities, better infrastructure, and a myriad of other liberties, such as schooling that, when available en masse, produces a well-educated population that is less susceptible to oppressive regimes. For example, while clean water may produce health benefits for people in India, it does little in the way of providing tangible needs for a nation growing exponentially, both in terms of population and technology.

Plus, if the economy is in shambles, there is no money to spend on the environment, say realists. You need to have a strong economy and make money before you can invest in long-term solutions for long-term problems like the environment. People in many nations cannot be concerned with preserving natural resources when they are trying to feed and protect their families. In 2011 World Bank president Robert Zoellick warned that more and more people around the world were being pushed into poverty by food prices, which one World Bank report claimed had increased by 36 percent in the previous year alone. Zoellick blamed the rapid increase on high fuel costs, bad harvests, and increased usage of foodstuffs on biofuel production.[10] Zoellick went on to say that this scenario is damaging, especially when it plays out in nations where the economy is not growing at a corresponding rate, thus creating an ever-widening gap that citizens cannot bridge. Many people in Senegal can only afford one meal a day, and even middle-class families in the Dakar suburbs are at risk of being driven into poverty in order to eat.[11]

Meanwhile, skeptics largely deny the existence of climate change, its potential impact on humankind, or, at the very least, humans' ability to impact it. Scientific research and observation show that global temperatures are cyclic and that the environment can and will fix itself over time. Fossil fuels and other resources are in no foreseeable danger of running out, especially as we develop new technologies that reveal deposits, and as we access those that have already been discovered.

Some skeptics also believe that environmental issues are merely masks for an anticapitalist, antidevelopment agenda and that environmentalist arguments are engineered to weaken what they see as a global plutocracy. This viewpoint especially rings true in the United States, where environmentalism has become associated with liberal political philosophies, including the environmental movement of the 1970s. At the same time, political conservatism in the United States has been linked to skepticism about global warming since the election of President Ronald Reagan in 1981 and his push for reduced governmental regulation.

However, American interest in conservation arose well before the election of Ronald Reagan. In 1892 the Sierra Club was established, and in 1916 the federal government created the National Park system. Smog was soon a factor in urban areas, and in the 1950s the first international air pollution conference took place.

By the late 1960s awareness had been piqued, ushering in a decade of cleanup with the birth of the Environmental Protection Agency. Concern mounted through the 1990s as scientists gathered evidence about the greenhouse effect and global warming.[12] By 2007 the environment was at the forefront of the international agenda, helped by news media and films like former vice president Al Gore's "An Inconvenient Truth." For thirty consecutive years, according to Gallup polls, Americans believed that the environment took precedence over economic growth, but when the global economic crisis struck in 2008, the economy took the lead for the first time. Public opinion reversed briefly following the 2010 oil spill in the Gulf of Mexico, but later in 2010 the environment was pushed to the background once again as Americans felt the lingering effects of the recession.[13]

In the United States, the prevailing message is not that individuals are against environmental protection but that it is an extravagance they are willing to forgo in order to make ends meet. The summer of 2011 presented a new economic crisis as the government faced the possibility of defaulting on its bills for the first time after hitting the Congress-imposed borrowing limit (debt ceiling) of $14.294 trillion. In the end, President Barack Obama was forced to accept a multitude of cuts to government spending in order to get Republicans to agree to a solution. The deal outlined a decade of across-the-board spending cuts that significantly affected several energy and environmental programs. According to Natural Resources Defense Council legislative director Scott Slesinger, everything from energy-efficiency grants to alternative fuels research and development, pollution monitoring, and the Environmental Protection Agency regulatory arm will be slashed as the government attempts to cut $2.7 trillion in spending.[14]

As the United States tries to cut spending, Brazil looks to thrive as a nation, and in Senegal the people merely want to survive. Around the world, governments are forced to make decisions that seem to put the environment and economy in opposition to one another. Faced with mounting debt, unemployment, and other imminent economic challenges, the question of whether environmental preservation should represent a top priority remains open for debate.

Notes

1. S. Wallace, "Farming the Amazon," *National Geographic Magazine*, January 2010, http://environment.nationalgeographic.com/environment/habitats/last-of-amazon/.
2. F. Pandolfi, "Voters Guide to Environmental Issues," *Popular Science*, November 1992, www.highbeam.com/doc/1G1-12810617.html.
3. Commonly credited as a Native American proverb.
4. H. Brooymans, "Tainted Water Lights Fire under Gas Fears," *Edmonton Journal*, December 13, 2005, www.canada.com/edmontonjournal/story.html?k=55507&id=798b13d1-adf0-41f6-bb3b-a02610475069.

5. "Environment and Society: Shell in the Community," Shell Nigeria, accessed October 22, 2013, www.shell.com.ng/home/content/nga /environment_society/shell_in_the_society/.

6. "Shell Admits Fueling Corruption," *BBC News*, last modified June 11, 2004, http://news.bbc.co .uk/go/pr/fr/-/2/hi/business/3796375.stm.

7. R. Costanza, R. D'Arge, R. de Groot, S. Farber, M. Grasso, B. Hannon, K. Limburg, S. Naeem, R. V. O'Neill, J. Paruelo, et al., "The Value of the World's Ecosystem Services and Natural Capital," *Nature* 387 (May 1997): 253–60.

8. Wallace, "Farming the Amazon."

9. J. Diamon, *Collapse: How Societies Choose to Fail or Succeed* (New York: Viking, 2005).

10. P. Inman, "Food Prices Pushing Millions into Extreme Poverty, World Bank Warns," *Guardian*, April 14, 2011, www.theguardian .com/business/2011/apr/14/food-price-inflation -world-bank-warning.

11. B. Diallo, "Price Hikes on Food Increases Problems in Senegal," *Deutcshe Welle World*, June 3, 2011, www.dw.de/price-hikes-on-food-increases -problems-in-senegal/a-15129266-1.

12. S. Krech, J. R. McNeill, and C. Merchant, *Encyclopedia of World Environmental History*, vol. 3 (New York: Routledge, 2004).

13. J. M. Jones, "Americans Increasingly Prioritize Economy over Environment," *Gallup*, March 17, 2011, www.gallup.com/poll/146681 /Americans-Increasingly-Prioritize-Economy -Environment.aspx.

14. D. Goode, "Energy Programs Prepare for Debt Deal Pain," *Politico*, August 1, 2011, www .politico.com/news/stories/0811/60399.html.

Checking Comprehension

A. Select the most appropriate answer for each question.

1. The purpose of the article is to
    a. illustrate the burning issue of environmental conservation with typical examples.
    b. provide the reader with arguments for economic development.
    c. persuade the reader to become environmentally conscious.
    d. explore reasons put forward by opposing sides in an economy-versus-environment debate.

2. The main idea of the article can be summarized as follows:
    a. Economic development is carried out at the expense of environmental conservation.
    b. Scientists generally agree that the exhaustion of natural resources threatens the survival of humankind.
    c. The issue of environmental conservation is open for debate due to pressing economic issues.
    d. Environmental conservation can be sacrificed for the sake of economic prosperity.

3. "Brazil has benefited from a growth-centric focus, but at a cost, some say." Based on this statement, what can you infer?
    a. Brazil faced a massive budget deficit owing to projects designed to improve its infrastructure.
    b. Many of Brazil's natural resources were damaged and depleted by reckless exploitation.
    c. As a result of compromising on welfare issues, the Brazilian government lost a significant percentage of its electorate.
    d. Brazil had to change its political structure in order to become the fastest-growing economy.

4. According to the article, environmentalists argue that
    a. economic development should be sacrificed for the sake of environmental protection.
    b. environmental issues require immediate attention in order to ensure a decent future for subsequent generations.
    c. humans already have exhausted their nonrenewable resources, the consequences of which are irreversible.
    d. all of the above.

5. The stance that realists take on the environment can be summed up as follows:
    a. Environmental problems are not worth spending money and time on since there are more pressing economic threats.
    b. A strong economy depends on a healthy environment, and vice versa; thus, both deserve careful attention.
    c. Economies generate valuable financial resources that, in turn, can be invested in the environment.
    d. None of the above.

6. Skeptics generally are opposed to environmental movements because they
    a. believe that environmental issues are overrated.
    b. think that everything that can be done to preserve the environment already has been done.
    c. support plutocracy.
    d. don't have enough power to influence decision makers.

7. As a nation, the United States historically has
    a. concerned itself more with the economy than the environment.
    b. taken extreme measures to protect the environment.
    c. fluctuated between emphasizing economic growth and environmental preservation.
    d. all of the above.

B. Complete the following sentences based on information from the text.

1. Brazilian rainforests offer economic opportunities such as . . .

    _____

2. According to environmentalists, preservation of the environment should take precedence because . . .

    _____

3. Some examples of large corporations impacting negatively on the environment of developing countries are . . .

    _____

4. Those who advocate primarily for economic growth maintain that . . .

    _____

5. The US position on the trade-off between economic growth and environmental protection can be described as . . .

    _____

Mastering Vocabulary

Active Vocabulary Collocations	
Economy & Environment	**General**
1. annual emissions	1. devastating impacts
2. community development	2. foreseeable future
3. conservation measures	3. imminent threat
4. employment opportunities	4. to bridge the gap
5. nonrenewable resources (vs. renewable resources)	5. long-term solutions
6. oil spills	6. mutually exclusive
7. to create jobs	7. open for debate
8. to cut (government) spending	8. pressing issue/preeminent concern
9. to exploit/to misuse/to abuse natural resources	9. to balance the two priorities
10. to generate revenue	10. to pose a problem
11. to prevent/to monitor pollution	11. to put something first
12. tangible benefits	12. to make ends meet
13. to raise people out of poverty	13. to take advantage of
14. to sustain economic growth	14. to take for granted
15. unique plant and animal species	15. to take precedence/priority

Expanding Vocabulary

A. Complete the mind maps begun in the pre-reading section by using active vocabulary collocations. In order to do this, you may need to expand your mind maps by adding new boxes and connections.

B. Fill in the sentences below with collocations from the Word Bank.

Word Bank		
oil spill	nonrenewable resources	generate revenue
create jobs	employment	tangible benefits
pose a problem	opportunities	take priority
monitor pollution	take for granted	
mutually exclusive	foreseeable future	

1. While drilling for crude oil, a large explosion caused a massive _____ that forever changed the fishing grounds and beaches.
2. Many believe the solution to unemployment is to increase government spending and thus _____ for many Americans.
3. Environmental protection and economic growth are not _____. Quite the contrary, we cannot have one without the other.
4. It is imperative that we become less dependent on _____ such as coal, petroleum, and natural gas and turn instead to more sustainable sources of energy.
5. Assuming current trends continue, our economic outlook appears bleak for the _____.
6. There is an increasing need for individuals working in the sciences; however, there are few _____ for those in the arts and humanities.
7. Global warming will _____ for animals living in the Arctic; many will potentially need to change where and what they eat.
8. Organic farmers are able to protect the environment from dangerous pesticides and still _____ by selling their crops in bulk to consumers through markets.
9. Planting trees in urban areas leads to _____, such as property value increases, and to intangible benefits, such as stress reduction.

C. ⊕ Select which one of the corresponding collocates is most commonly used with each vocabulary word. To do this, go to (http://corpus.byu.edu/coca/) and type the vocabulary word in the WORD(S) box and then click on COLLOCATES. (You do not need to type anything in the COLLOCATES box that appears.) Under SORTING AND LIMITS find the dropdown menu next to MINIMUM and select MUTUAL INFO. Click SEARCH.

Economy & Conservation	Corresponding Collocates			
1. Annual	a. growth	b. issue	c. income	d. salary
2. Devastating	a. impact	b. damage	c. pollution	d. disease
3. Nonrenewable	a. emissions	b. debate	c. resources	d. problem
4. Economic	a. challenges	b. revenue	c. reform	d. exclusion
5. Mounting	a. advantages	b. costs	c. gaps	d. emissions
6. Imminent	a. growth	b. impact	c. resources	d. danger
7. Unique	a. oil spills	b. species	c. debt	d. challenges
8. Pressing	a. impact	b. issues	c. threat	d. Republicans
9. Lax	a. disaster	b. crisis	c. benefits	d. regulations
10. Conserve	a. energy	b. impacts	c. debt	d. revenue

D. Choose five collocations concerning the economy and conservation from the previous activity. Write a sentence for each collocation that either supports or condemns illegal logging in Brazil, as described in the article.

Exploring the Meaning

Language Note 2

Verbs are called *transitive* if they can be followed by a *direct object*, such as "to make something, to break something, to lose something." *Intransitive* verbs *cannot* be followed by a *direct object*, as in "to rise, to die, to smile." Both transitive and intransitive verbs might be followed by an *indirect object*, which implies the use of a preposition, as in the model: VERB + PREPOSITION + NOUN

A. Circle the transitive verbs in the paragraph below.

The economy never thrives unless people determine to save not only money but also the environment. Trees, for instance, provide us with boards for building, books for reading, and wood for burning. Trees benefit everyone but are in limited supply. If we want to continue to prosper, we must protect and conserve this valuable resource. We need to create a plan that estimates how much deforestation can be allowed before we generate too many problems for trees and the animals that rely upon them. We must preserve Mother Nature's delicate balance.

B. Create collocations of your own by drawing from five transitive verbs from the previous paragraph and the nouns below. Ex: to save goods.

value, growth, resources, goods, money, ideas, profit, outcome, results, needs, nature, profit, income, success, risks, revenue

1. _____
2. _____
3. _____
4. _____
5. _____

C. Using these collocations, construct five questions to challenge your partner's assigned opinion regarding the economy-versus-environment debate.

D. Match collocations from the text with their meanings

1.	to be open for debate	a.	to cause a setback
2.	to take precedence	b.	to fail to properly appreciate
3.	to cash in on	c.	to be of the highest importance
4.	to pose a problem	d.	to fail to have an evident solution
5.	to put something first	e.	to give priority to something
6.	to take for granted	f.	to take advantage of

E. Paraphrase the following sentences using the collocations from the left column in the previous table.
   1. We rarely appreciate the biodiversity that is still left on our planet.
   2. Some governments place too much importance on the economy and ignore pressing environmental problems.
   3. Many entrepreneurs try to benefit from what can often be lax regulations regarding the use of natural resources.
   4. Environmental conservation only becomes a government's top priority during catastrophic events such as massive oil spills.
   5. In times of a serious economic crisis, government officials generally must choose between short-term and long-term welfare.
   6. The issue of tax cuts for small businesses still arouses heated discussions.

F. Using active vocabulary collocations, propose solutions to the problems addressed in the first three sentences above.

Discussing the Article

A. Working with a partner, use active vocabulary collocations to answer the following questions based on the text.
   1. Judging by the example of the Amazon, does government interference contribute to environmental preservation in the area?
   2. Why is balancing the interests of economic growth and environmental conservation "easier said than done?" Do you agree? Why or why not?

3. According to the text, environmentalists believe that the human race is "at the peak of cultural and technological growth." In what ways is this statement true? False?

4. Should governments be more concerned with short-term or long-term effects on the environment from economic growth?

5. If deforestation is so detrimental to the environment, why does it continue to occur? What would stop it?

6. How do skeptics differ from realists in their support of economic growth and criticism of environmentalism?

7. How should governments determine what constitutes environmental damage?

8. Should public opinion affect policy decisions relevant to the economy and the environment? Why or why not?

9. Realists claim that the only way a government can properly care for the environment is first to develop its economy. How is the example of the United States' default scare evidence to the contrary?

10. How has the debate over balancing environmental preservation and economic growth been resolved in your country?

Constructing Critical Discourse

Recognizing Euphemisms

Note   Euphemisms commonly appear in official media and promote political correctness by downplaying unpleasant facts through the use of subtle wording. Recognizing euphemisms can sometimes be challenging for a nonnative speaker, so learning which ones exist in spoken language is important.

A. Identify the euphemism in each sentence. To do so, find the words and expressions that represent less subtle equivalents for the following notions: *disaster, unemployed, cheap, to exploit land, poor*.

1. A large corporation developed vast areas of the rainforest.

2. The incident in the Gulf region led to job loss.

3. When allocating financial resources for the preservation of the local ecosystem, the new governor was being economical.

4. Emerging nations have to rely on handouts from international organizations.

5. During the financial crisis, a lot of people found themselves between jobs.

Forming Hypotheses

A. Study the following quotation from an article published in the *New York Times* titled "The New Sputnik" (2009), by Thomas L. Friedman.[1] Identify similarities between China and the Soviet Union.

> I believe this Chinese decision to go green is the 21st-century equivalent of the Soviet Union's 1957 launch of Sputnik. . . . And when China decides it has to go green out of necessity, watch out. You will not just be buying your toys from China. You will buy your next electric car, solar panels, batteries and energy-efficiency software from China.

B. Using the pattern shown below for constructing hypotheses, respond to the following questions regarding the Friedman quote.

Future condition	+	Possible future consequences
• If something **happens**, • When something **happens**, • If something **is done**, • When something **is done**,	→	• something **will happen**. • something **might happen**. • something **could happen**. • something **may happen**.

1. What environmental consequences will China's aspiration to go green have on the global community?
2. What negative effects could such a decision have on the world economy?
3. What benefits to the global community could result from such a decision?
4. What challenges might China face in the process of achieving this goal?

Practice Debate

A. Choose one of the roles below and role-play it using at least ten active vocabulary collocations per person.

---

1. Thomas Friedman, "The New Sputnik," *New York Times*, September 26, 2009, http://www.nytimes.com /2009/09/27/opinion/27friedman.html?_r=0.

Dialogue 1

<u>Role A:</u> A candidate aiming to win a seat in the local government by being a green activist.

<u>Role B:</u> A representative emphasizing economic development in the community.

Dialogue 2

<u>Role A:</u> A federal government official trying to eliminate the budget deficit.

<u>Role B:</u> Green lobbyists trying to get more money for renewable energy research.

Dialogue 3

<u>Role A:</u> A representative of a large corporation trying to open a subsidiary in a new area.

<u>Role B:</u> Rallying locals who are more interested in preserving the region's unique ecosystem.

Listening

Pre-Listening

A. Before listening to the audio file, predict the arguments that you'll hear. Fill in the table below.

Environmental conservation should not be carried out at the expense of economic growth.	Economic growth cannot serve as an excuse for environmental deterioration.
•	•
•	•
•	•
•	•
•	•
•	•

🎧 While Listening

A. **Listening for general comprehension:** Listen to audio file 1.2 and put a check next to arguments that appear in the table. Write down additional arguments that initially were missing in your table.

B. **Listening for specific details:** Listen to the audio file a second time and evaluate the arguments you listed in the table above as "strong" or "weak." Propose ways of improving the arguments you labeled as "weak."

Post-Listening

A. Which side do you think presented a more persuasive argument? Support your opinion by citing their strongest argument.

B. In every debate, someone has the last word. Predict what the opposing side's response would be to the final argument you heard.

Formatting the Argument: Writing

How to Write a Position Paper: Planning Content

A position paper, like a debate, argues one side of an issue. Your job is to convince your audience that your opinion is defensible. Before writing a position paper, carefully consider its contents. You must address multiple aspects of an issue and present it in a way that is easy for your audience to understand. To convince the audience that your claims are valid and that the opposing side's counterclaims are not, you must support your argument with persuasive evidence.

Evidence: Before writing your position paper, do some research on the topic. Begin with a list of claims and counterclaims and consider how to support or refute each. Supporting information includes the following:

Type of Information	Type of Source
general overview	directories, encyclopedias, almanacs
in-depth studies	books, government reports
scholarly findings	academic journals
case studies	newspapers, magazines
statistics	government agencies and associations
research	association and institute reports

A. Identify several potential sources for your position paper. Choose multiple types of sources, for example, encyclopedias, scholarly articles, and newspaper articles. List your sources here.

_____

_____

B. Read the following position paper critically and answer the questions below:
   1. Does the author make any assumptions? If so, what are the assumptions?
   2. What kind of proof does the author offer for her assertions?
   3. What additional information would you include to strengthen the claims?

Environment versus Economy: Position Paper

Environmental conservation and economic growth rarely go hand in hand. While balancing the interests of both a strong economy and a healthy environment represents a noble goal, accomplishing such a task is easier said than done. Accordingly, environmental conservation should not be carried out at the expense of economic growth, particularly in nations with struggling economies.

A comparison of polling data from 2008 and 2013 indicated that Americans were concerned more about the economy than the environment after the 2008 recession.[1] In 2008, 49 percent of those surveyed reported that the environment should take precedence over the economy with only 42 percent of people prioritizing the environment. By 2013 these numbers had reversed, with 48 percent of people favoring the economy and only 43 percent putting the environment first. Struggling economies precipitate joblessness and poverty and likely triggered this shift in priorities. People cannot be expected to place environmental concerns over feeding and protecting their families.

While the environment is important, the effects of a bad economy significantly affect people's daily lives. In some third-world countries, people cannot afford to buy food, let alone help the environment. For example, in Senegal, some people can only afford one meal a day, and even middle-class families in the Dakar suburbs spend a disproportionate percentage of their money just to eat.[2] Conversely, a strong economy contributes to increased employment opportunities, better infrastructure, and an array of social benefits, such as public education and health care.

Proponents of environmental protection argue that climate change contributes to increased food prices and, therefore, that protecting the environment benefits both individuals and the economy. Such price increases, in turn, affect the rest of the economy because when people pay more for food, they spend less on everything else.[3] Therefore, the greater the impact of climate change on food production, the more the global economy suffers.

However, even if such an argument holds true, evidence suggests that some nations prosper when focusing on economic growth rather than the environment. For instance, the Brazilian government and private entities in Brazil have cut into the Amazon with dams, power lines, and oil and gas pipelines, all in the name of economic growth, but the Brazilian economy represents one of the fastest-growing economies in the world, and the standard of living for people there continues to

improve.[4] Although conservation efforts are important, the health of the economy takes precedence over the health of trees.

Furthermore, past experience shows that nations can spend money on the environment with little to no effect. In 2006 Canada spent billions of dollars on climate initiatives in an attempt to reduce greenhouse emissions. Nevertheless, output of greenhouse gasses did not decrease; rather, it rose to 122 percent beyond the set goal.[5] To add insult to injury, the economy took a turn for the worse shortly thereafter. Thus, money spent on the environment did not have its intended effect and might have been better spent protecting the economy against a downturn. Ideally, countries could balance economic growth and environmental protection, but ultimately, economic growth takes priority. Moreover, if we really want to protect our planet, focusing on the economy will ensure sufficient resources necessary to realize this goal.

In conclusion, while the environment is important, protecting it at the cost of economic growth is a luxury that many countries cannot afford. Nations should give top priority to strengthening the economy in order to protect individuals from the ills of joblessness and poverty and to subsidize efforts to preserve the environment.

Notes

1. L. Saad, "More Americans Still Prioritize Economy over Environment," *Gallup*, April 3, 2013, www.gallup.com/poll/161594/americans-prioritize-economy-environment.aspx.

2. B. Diallo, "Price Hikes on Food Increases Problems in Senegal," *Deutcshe Welle World*, June 3, 2011, www.dw.de/price-hikes-on-food-increases-problems-in-senegal/a-15129266-1.

3. I. Carey, "The Great Economy Versus Environment Myth," *Huffington Post*, April 5, 2012, www.huffingtonpost.com/ian-carey/the-great-economy-versus-_b_1398439.html.

4. S. Wallace, "Farming the Amazon," *National Geographic Magazine*, January 2010, http:// environment.nationalgeographic.com /environment/habitats/last-of-amazon/; and

"Brazil Overview," *World Bank*, accessed October 22, 2013, www.worldbank.org/en/country /brazil/overview.

5. D. Owen, "Economy vs. Environment," *New Yorker*, March 30, 2009, www.newyorker .com/talk/comment/2009/03/30/090330taco _talk_owen.

Write Your Own Position Paper

A. Write a position paper on the topic of "economy versus environment" that consists of five to six paragraphs. Be sure to include active vocabulary collocations from this unit.

Formatting the Argument: Speaking

Implementing Rhetorical Strategies

A. Study the following note:

> **Strategy Note 1**   Like a game of chess, there are different strategies that can be used when we debate someone. The Greek philosophers suggested at least five strategies. They are listed below in the form of questions that could be used as part of a debate strategy.

1. Conjecture (What if . . . ?) questions: What would happen if we gave top priority to economic development all the time in all situations?
2. Definition questions: What does "environment" mean? Are humans as much a part of the "environment" as animals and the weather?
3. Cause and consequence questions: What are the likely results of an increase in global temperatures?
4. Value questions: Do human beings have a responsibility to protect the environment, such as the Brazilian rainforest, even at the expense of improving human life?
5. Procedural questions: How do we develop an approach to sustainability that both protects the environment and helps nations develop economically?

In this unit, we will focus on the first strategy: **the conjecture argument.** This is where you propose a hypothetical, or "what if, then" statement that is a positive logical extension of your position, or a negative logical extension of the other side.

B. Review the text highlighting important words or phrases that you could use to support your side of the debate. For example, if you are arguing that economic development should be given greater priority over environmental protection, you may want to concentrate on statements that discuss what would happen if we gave greater priority to environmental concerns over economic development.

List five important conjectures that support your side of the argument.

1. _____
2. _____
3. _____
4. _____
5. _____

C. During the debate, you can use these conjectures to support your argument or to weaken the argument of the other side. For instance, you could ask and answer something like, "What difference does it make if people and nations are 'wealthy,' if we are all living in a man-made environment that is hostile to human beings?"

Based on the conjectures you have listed above, write five sentences or questions you could use in your debate.

1. _____
2. _____
3. _____
4. _____
5. _____

D. As you prepare for the debate, you can predict that the other side will use conjectures that support their side of the argument. You can argue against these conjectures by pointing out weaknesses in their hypotheses or the consequences of these hypotheses. To illustrate, the other side may argue that if we don't do something about global warming, human civilization will be threatened. You could argue that history has shown that human civilizations flourish when the climate warms.

Review the text and list five key conjectures that the other side could use in their side of the debate. Then list how you would argue against these conjectures.

1. _____
2. _____
3. _____
4. _____
5. _____

Framing Templates

A.   The following expressions can be used to **introduce the issue**. Review these framing templates and incorporate them into both your oral and written arguments.

    1. It's common knowledge that . . .

    2. Many people tend to think that . . .

    3. It's common sense that . . .

    4. It is often believed that . . .

    5. Everyone would agree that . . .

Dealing with Questions

A.   There may be times during the debate when you need to **acknowledge questions**. Use the following statements in case this situation arises.

- Thank you for your question. I see what you are saying. However, . . .
- I completely agree with you on . . . , but I am afraid I cannot provide you with that information as . . .
- Right. Your question is clear, but . . .
- That definitely is an important issue, but . . .
- Thank you for bringing it up, but . . .
- Thank you for raising this issue, but . . .
- I appreciate your bringing it up, but . . .

Speaking

A.   **Oral Presentation:** Prepare a three- to five-minute oral presentation arguing your position. After practicing, record your presentation and then listen to it. What areas do you need to improve on? Be prepared to give your presentation in class.

B.   **Debate:** Now it's time for you to debate. Synthesize all your notes dealing with arguments, useful active vocabulary collocations, and framing templates to assist you during the actual debate. Remember that these will serve as a reference only, not as a text to be read directly during your debate.

Reflection

Self-Evaluation

A. Think back over the work you have done thus far. Plot your responses to the following statements on the scale.

1. I felt prepared to debate this topic.
2. I was motivated to debate this topic.
3. I put a lot of effort into preparing to debate this topic.

1	2	3	4	5	6
Completely Agree	Agree	Somewhat Agree	Somewhat Disagree	Disagree	Completely Disagree

B. If most of your answers were at the right end of the spectrum, what can you do to move to the left end? If most of your answers were at the left end of the spectrum, what can you do to stay in that area?

Vocabulary Recall

Identify **ten** active vocabulary collocations you have learned and used in this chapter that you feel were most beneficial to you as you debated.

1. _____
2. _____
3. _____
4. _____
5. _____
6. _____
7. _____
8. _____
9. _____
10. _____

Interventionism versus Isolationism

Spreading Democracy or Breaching Sovereignty

Pre-Reading

Introducing the Issue

A. With a partner discuss the following questions using the photographs and corresponding descriptions.

Two girls gossip about an outcast girl. (Credit: Beth Van Trees)

After class, two friends get in an argument. (Credit: Aaron Tait. https://creativecommons.org/licenses/by/2.0/)

A young man finds out that he's lost his job. (Credit: Dana Skolnick. https://creativecommons.org/licenses/by-nd/2.0/)

1. In which of these situations do you think people would most likely intervene? Why?
2. What factors do you think determine whether or not individuals would offer assistance to those shown in the pictures?
3. In your opinion, are we obligated to help others only when they ask or any time we notice that they need assistance? Defend your opinion.
4. Tell your partner about a time when you assisted someone who did not ask you to do so. How did that person respond to your assistance?

B. Study **Language Note 1** on the meaning of the words "democracy" and "sovereignty" presented through examples and synonyms (provided by the *Oxford American Dictionary and Thesaurus*) and paraphrase the title "Spreading Democracy or Breaching Sovereignty" by substituting these words with their synonyms.

Language Note 1		
	Democracy	**Sovereignty**
Meaning	A system of government by the whole population of all the eligible members of a state, typically through elected representatives.	The authority of a state to govern itself.
Example	"A democracy in that country likely will not come about any time soon."	"The colony demanded full sovereignty."
Synonyms	representative government, elective government, self-government, government by the people	autonomy, independence, self-government, self-rule, home rule, self-determination, freedom
Antonyms	dictatorship	subjugation
Difference	The difference in meaning between "democracy" and "sovereignty" is that democracy implies freedom from dictatorship *within* a country while sovereignty implies freedom from *outside* control.	

C. Analyze the title "Spreading Democracy or Breaching Sovereignty."
   1. How would you characterize the relationship between the two processes of "spreading democracy" and "breaching sovereignty?"
   2. Do you think these processes (a) contradict each other, (b) complement each other, or (c) parallel each other? Explain your thinking.

D. Based on the title "Spreading Democracy or Breaching Sovereignty," make a list of issues that might appear in the article.
   1. foreign intervention
   2. _____

3. _____

4. _____

5. _____

Creating Mind Maps

A. Brainstorm as many words as you know associated with the challenges a country might face in its domestic and foreign affairs. Arrange your ideas to create two separate mind maps according to the pattern shown below. After reading the article, you will be able to add more information, so leaving boxes blank at this point is okay.

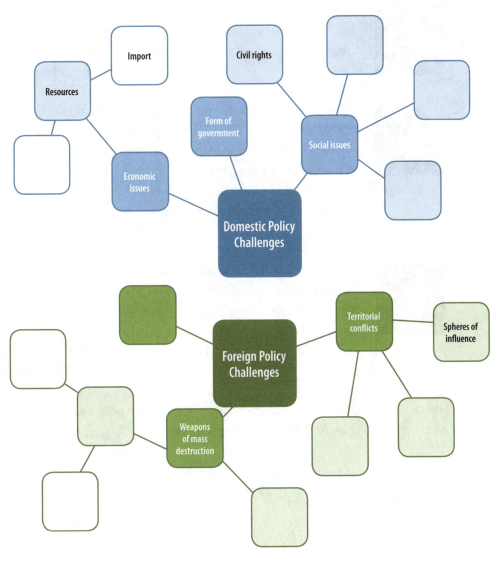

B. Compare your maps with those of your classmates to generate additional ideas. After completing each of the two maps, decide which topic areas can help bridge the gap between the two maps. In other words, which issues concerning domestic and foreign policy challenges intersect?

Discussing Facts and Opinions

A. Read the quotations by American presidents on US foreign policy. Find words dealing with foreign policy challenges that can be added to the mind maps.

Equal and exact justice to all men, of whatever state or persuasion, religious or political; peace, commerce, and honest friendship with all nations, entangling alliances with none.

Thomas Jefferson

We must face the fact that the United States is neither omnipotent nor omniscient; that we are only 6 percent of the world's population; that we cannot impose our will upon the other 94 percent of mankind; that we cannot right every wrong or reverse every adversity; and that therefore there cannot be an American solution to every world problem.

John Fitzgerald Kennedy

There is no longer a clear, bright line dividing America's domestic concerns and America's foreign policy concerns. . . . If we want America to stay on the right track, if we want other people to be on that track and have the chance to enjoy peace and prosperity, we have no choice but to try to lead the train.

Bill Clinton

B. Summarize each quotation to explain what American foreign policy was like during the administration of each of the respective presidents.

Studying the Topic

Focused Reading

A. As you read "Spreading Democracy or Breaching Sovereignty," list the arguments for both sides of the debate in the following table.

Interventionism	Isolationism
•	•
•	•
•	•
•	•
•	•
•	•
•	•
•	•
•	•
•	•

B. Check your pronunciation of unfamiliar words from the text as you listen to Audio Recording 2.1.

Spreading Democracy or Breaching Sovereignty

Grant Newman

The Arab Spring of 2011 caught the world off guard. As citizens clashed with their long-standing, often antiquated leaders, and as government after government fell in a domino effect of power changes, it became increasingly clear that the consequences could have a lasting effect well beyond the Middle East region. A pending civil war in Libya that threatened the lives of civilians eventually proved to be the last straw for several Western countries, namely, France, Britain, and the United States, who proceeded to draft a United Nations resolution that would sanction intervention by foreign governments. In the wake of this resolution, the world has been discussing whether foreign governments are justified in intervening in the domestic affairs of sovereign countries or whether countries have a fundamental right to self-determination that is free of foreign intervention.

Not the least convincing of reasons for foreign countries to intervene in the domestic affairs of sovereign countries is the prevention of crimes against humanity, especially genocide. Samantha Power, a Harvard professor who focuses on human rights, declared in *A Problem From Hell* (2002) that "stopping the execution of thousands of foreigners [is], in some cases, worth the cost in dollars, troops, and strained alliances."[1] The moral grounds invoked by Power for such intervention are articulated in the United Nations' *Convention on the Prevention and Punishment of the Crime of Genocide*, which states that such atrocities are so unacceptable in a civilized world that sovereignty must be breached in order to avoid them. Approved during the aftermath of World War II and the horrors of the Holocaust, this document officially condemns genocide as a crime and allows member nations to request that the United Nations take action "as they consider appropriate" in order to prevent and suppress acts of genocide.

Thus, in addition to moral grounds, legal grounds also exist for countries to interfere in the domestic affairs of other countries in order to spare the lives of countless innocents.

Foreign countries might also justify intervention in a sovereign's affairs when consequences become systemic—that is, when a sovereign's internal problems begin to have external consequences. Somalia is a failed state. A power vacuum within the country has led to a government that is incapable of dealing with an insurgency in which about nine thousand citizens were killed in 2008 alone.[2] Even worse, according to Ahmedou Ould Abdallah, the United Nations' envoy to the country, "Somalia is a victim of its political, business and military elite. They've taken the country hostage."[3] Yet the failure of the Somali state is felt abroad as well.

In 2010 Somali pirates took 1,181 people hostage. Ransoms paid amounted to $238 million, or $5.4 million per ship— a massive increase from a comparatively meager $150,000 per ship in 2005, suggesting that, unattended, the situation only worsened.[4] Jack Lang, a UN advisor on piracy, estimates the total economic costs of piracy at $5 billion to $7 billion per year.[5] Taking these figures into account, Somalia's onshore lawlessness appears to manifest itself in offshore piracy that threatens many noncitizens. Developing the failed state, which includes ceasing all offshore dumping and thereby offering greater prospects to Somalis, is considered to be the most effective remedy to the problem;[6] onshore opportunities ought to appear more attractive than offshore piracy. Little wonder, then, that many international coalitions, such as the American-led CTF-151, have been formed to deal with the problem of piracy. The deployment of Chinese, Indian, Japanese, and Russian naval forces, among others, under national command to patrol the waters surrounding Somalia is no more surprising.[7]

Counterarguments to intervention abound. Mainly, countries ought to respect the sovereignty and territorial integrity of fellow countries if they expect fellow countries to do likewise. China and Russia are key advocates of this position, logically claiming that, because they would not want others to meddle in their internal affairs, they should not meddle in the affairs of others. This eastern tandem cited its "golden rule" policy by abstaining, along with three other countries, from the vote to ratify the UN resolution on intervention in Libya. These countries have also been quick to express their disappointment regarding the actions taken in Libya, with a spokesman for the Russian Foreign Ministry "calling on the respective states to halt the indiscriminate use of force."[8]

Opponents to intervention further argue that it is simply not in the interest of a foreign country. Robert Gates, the US defense secretary until July 1, 2011, opposed intervention in Libya, thinking that it would not be in the United States' vital interests—that the United States would have little to gain from intervention and potentially much to lose.[9] Lack of sufficient interest is especially significant when diverted resources could find good use at home. Case in point, Joseph Stiglitz and Linda Bilmes, professors at Columbia University and Harvard University, respectively, opining for the *Washington Post* on September 5, 2010, priced the Iraq War at $3 trillion for the United States since its inception in 2003. Such a sum of money might have proven useful for domestic spending in the United States, especially considering the economic recession that hit the United States in the latter part of the decade. In retrospect, people might question whether intervention in Iraq truly fell within the bounds of US interests.

US policy was not always biased toward intervention. John Quincy Adams, an early US president, once stated, "America does not go abroad in search of monsters to destroy. She is the well-wisher to freedom and independence of all, [but the] champion and vindicator only of her own."[10] The Monroe Doctrine, adopted in 1832, called for Europe to cease colonizing the Americas. In return, the United States would not meddle in the affairs of existing European colonies or states. The adoption of the Monroe Doctrine coincided with many Latin American countries declaring their independence from the Spanish crown and, accordingly, attempted to prevent other European colonizers from filling the post-Spain void. The United States thereby constructed an isolationist wall between the Old World and the New World, although it did proceed to intervene in the Americas and Pacific Islands. Nevertheless, isolation from Europe lasted almost a hundred years until Woodrow

Wilson established the League of Nations following World War I. From that point forward, the United States' ostensible bias against interventionism died.

The embodiment of contemporary US interventionism might very well be what is known as the Bush Doctrine, named after former US president George W. Bush, which describes an idealist policy of acting based on moral imperatives. In this framework, action against Iraq was justified as a preemptive war that would both spread democracy—an ideal—and topple a regime that posed a potential threat to world security in general, and that of the United States in particular. But such preemption is risky. Prior to the US invasion of Iraq, George F. Keenan, a US diplomat, stated in 2002, "Today, if we went into Iraq, as [President Bush] would like us to do, you know where you begin. You never know where you are going to end."[11] Such idealism has cost American taxpayers $3 trillion.

A natural reaction from Barack Obama's administration to Bush's idealism would be a retreat toward realism—a return to acting cautiously and according to national interests as opposed to ideals. However, as a young senator, Obama, perhaps fatefully, invited Samantha Power to be a foreign policy fellow in his office, bringing with her the opinion that, due to

an inherent lack of information regarding the likelihood of atrocity being committed, US presidents "must have a bias toward belief that massacres are imminent."[12] It is no wonder, then, that Obama supported intervention in Libya, especially in response to Muammar Gaddafi, Libya's dictator, calling domestic opponents of his regime cockroaches—a term used by Hutus to describe Tutsis during the Rwandan genocide.[13] Yet by no means did Obama default to his predecessor's quixotism, preferring instead to enter into a UN-sanctioned coalition that even included Arab states: true multilateralism, in the words of Obama, or, in the words of many of his supporters from the American left, the Anti-Bush Doctrine.[14]

The world will never know how Libya's rebels would have fared without Western intervention. The volatile nature of events in the region allowed one to anticipate any number of possibilities. Part of the world will praise the aversion to a potential humanitarian atrocity, while still another part will condemn the encroachment of true sovereignty. Perhaps no overlying policy exists, suggesting that foreign countries must make decisions on a case-by-case basis. Ultimately, the burden of proof lies with intervening countries. Their success in lifting this burden is for the court of public opinion to judge.

Notes

1. Quoted in Ryan Lizza, "The Consequential-ist: How the Arab Spring Remade Obama's Foreign Policy," *New Yorker*, May 2, 2011, www .newyorker.com/reporting/2011/05/02/110502fa _fact_lizza.

2. "Somalia: The World's Most Utterly Failed State," *Economist*, October 2, 2008, www .economist.com/node/12342212.

3. Ibid.

4. "Somali Piracy: At Sea," *Economist*, February 3, 2011, www.economist.com/node/18070160.

5. Ibid.

6. Ibid.

7. "Piracy: No Stopping Them," *Economist*, February 3, 2011, www.economist.com/node /18061574.

8. Quoted in Martin Beckford, "Libya Attacks Criticized by Arab League, China, Russia and India," *Telegraph*, March 21, 2011, www.telegraph.co.uk/news/worldnews /africaandindianocean/libya/8393950/Libya -attacks-criticised-by-Arab-League-China -Russia-and-India.html.

9. Lizza, "Consequentialist."

10. Ibid.

11. Ibid.

12. Ibid.

13. "Responsibility to Protect: The Lessons of Libya," *Economist*, May 19, 2011, www .economist.com/node/18709571.

14. David Corn, "Libya: Obama Crafts the Anti-Bush Doctrine," *Mother Jones*, March 18, 2011, www.motherjones.com/politics/2011/03/libya -obama-anti-bush-doctrine.

Checking Comprehension

A. Based on the text, indicate whether each statement is true or false. Modify false statements to make them true.

1. Recent dissatisfaction with long-standing leaders, which has led to power changes in several countries, is likely to have a lasting regional effect only.

2. Prevention of crimes against humanity, for example, genocide, represents one of the most convincing arguments for why foreign governments ought to avoid intervention.

3. Foreign intervention can be justified when the ramifications of an internal policy affect neighboring countries.

4. The Eastern tandem (China, Russia) cited the "golden rule" to justify intervention in the internal affairs of other countries.

5. The resources spent in Iraq might have proven useful for domestic spending in the United States.

6. The volatile nature of the Libyan conflict enabled one to anticipate a fixed number of possible outcomes.

7. The author of this article suggests that foreign countries should make foreign policy decisions on a case-by-case basis.

Mastering Vocabulary

Active Vocabulary Collocations	
Foreign and Domestic Affairs	**General**
1. civil war	1. a remedy to the problem
2. human rights	2. key advocates of this position
3. regime change	3. moral/legal/economic grounds
4. to be in somebody's vital interests	4. to be biased toward/against something
5. to breach sovereignty	5. to be the last straw
6. to commit atrocities	6. to catch somebody off guard
7. to condemn something as a crime	7. to consider something appropriate
8. to deploy armed forces	8. to deal with the problem
9. to enter an international coalition/ alliance	9. to fall within the bounds of
10. to meddle in internal affairs	10. to have a fundamental right
11. to sanction intervention	11. to have a lasting effect
12. to prevent genocide	12. to manifest itself in something
13. to respect territorial integrity	13. to pose a threat
14. to justify intervention	14. to take action
15. to spread democracy	15. to take something into account

Expanding Vocabulary

A. Complete the mind maps begun in the pre-reading section by using active vocabulary collocations above. In order to do this, you may need to expand your mind maps by adding new boxes and connections.

B. Fill in the missing prepositions after the nouns.
 1. The world financial crisis produced an enormous effect _____ emerging economies.
 2. The inalienable rights listed in the Declaration of Independence include the right _____ life, liberty, and the pursuit of happiness.
 3. Terrorists pose a threat _____ global security.
 4. The global community usually condemns crimes _____ ethnic minorities.
 5. Tightening borders might serve as a remedy _____ the problem of illegal immigration.

C. Fill in the sentences below with items from the Word Bank.

Word Bank		
fundamental right	independence	vital interests
democracy	genocide	armed forces
international alliance	atrocities	regime change
civil war	territorial integrity	intervention

 1. Free speech is a _____ in the United States, meaning people are entitled to say what they want.
 2. When the country declared its _____, it was finally free from outside control.
 3. The leader took full credit for the many _____ but claimed that such cruel injustices were common in war.
 4. In the interest of creating an _____, the countries cooperated so that everyone would be free from danger.
 5. As long as the pirates did not constitute a major threat to its _____, Rome paid little attention to them.
 6. He called for the _____ of Georgia to be respected because he did not want to change the borders of the country.

7. He felt it was necessary to join the _____ because he wanted to defend his country from enemies.

8. The people do not support the current form of government and feel it is time for a _____.

9. No one thought a _____ was possible; however, the citizens of Bosnia fought one another without hesitation.

10. Though the government did not want to meddle in state affairs, federal _____ was necessary in order to ensure that citizens were protected.

D. Go to COCA (http://corpus.byu.edu/coca/) and find three collocations commonly used in conjunction with the following words. To do this, type the word in the WORD(s) box and then type "[v*]" in the COLLOCATES box. Under SORTING AND LIMITS find the dropdown menu next to MINIMUM and select MUTUAL INFO. Type each collocation in the WORD(S) box and click SEARCH.

Foreign & Domestic Affairs	Corresponding Collocates		
1. Resolution	a. adopt	b. pass	c. authorize
2. Coalition			
3. Intervention			
4. Genocide			
5. Democracy			
6. Atrocities			
7. Territorial integrity			
8. Independence			
9. Civil war			
10. Armed forces			

E. Choose five collocations concerning foreign and domestic affairs from the previous activity. Write a sentence for each collocation that describes foreign and/or domestic affairs in your home country.

1. _____
2. _____
3. _____
4. _____
5. _____

Exploring the Meaning

A. Fill in the table below by grouping active vocabulary collocations according to their connotation.

Positive	Context-Dependent	Negative
•	•	•
•	•	•
•	•	•
•	•	•
•	•	•
•	•	•
•	•	•

B. Study the following definitions of interventionism and isolationism.
Interventionism refers to a policy of nondefensive or proactive activity undertaken by a nation-state to manipulate another country's government. It may involve activities such as threat of war, assassination of government or military leaders, and economic embargoes of all descriptions.
Isolationism describes a political doctrine that holds that political rulers should avoid entangling alliances with other nations and avoid all wars not related to direct territorial defenses. In modern contexts, it can also employ economic protectionism.

C. Identify words from the list of active vocabulary collocations that relate to the two policies and list them under "Interventionism" and "Isolationism" in the following table.

Interventionism	Isolationism
•	•
•	•
•	•
•	•
•	•
•	•
•	•
•	•
•	•
•	•

D. Many of the active vocabulary collocates you listed in the table in C have similar and opposing meanings. For each word below in column A, find a synonym in column B and an antonym in column C.

A	B	C
1. to sanction	a. supporter	A. foreign
2. sovereignty	b. essential	B. withdrawal
3. to respect	c. to place	C. opponent
4. vital	d. intervention	D. to desecrate
5. invasion	e. domestic	E. to condemn
6. to deploy	f. to approve	F. to withdraw
7. internal	g. autonomy	G. dependency
8. advocate	h. to honor	H. minor

E. Brainstorm possible endings to the following sentences and incorporate any of the
    words in the previous two activities.
    1. Continual meddling in other countries' internal affairs eventually leads to . . .

    _____

    2. The countries began cooperating with one another in order to . . .

    _____

    3. A feeling of vulnerability is now common in public places because . . .

    _____

    4. Double standards mean that some countries are allowed to disregard the territo-
        rial integrity of others, while other countries . . .

    _____

    5. Some UN members condemned intervention despite the fact that . . .

    _____

F. Read the imaginary scenario below.

        The president of Country X notices that the citizens of nearby Country Y are
        not allowed to vote for leaders or laws. The president of Country X wants to
        deploy armed forces to fix this injustice and asks you for advice.

    Use the active vocabulary collocations from the Interventionism and Isolationism
    table above to advise the president on what to do. Partner 1 favors isolation while Part-
    ner 2 favors intervention; present your arguments accordingly.
        Ex. *"I believe we need to respect the autonomy of Country Y because . . ."*

Discussing the Article

A. Working with a partner, use active vocabulary collocations to answer the following
    questions based on the text.
    1. Why would countries outside of the African region become involved in the affairs
        of African countries?
    2. What risks do foreign countries take when becoming involved in human rights
        issues that only indirectly affect citizens in their own countries?
    3. How does the "failed state" of Somalia affect foreign nations?
    4. Why would China, India, Japan, and Russia employ their naval forces to prevent
        Somali piracy?
    5. Why is it sometimes in a country's best interest to refrain from meddling in
        another country's internal affairs?

6. Did US intervention in Iraq further the interests of the United States? Why or why not?

7. Which is a better guide in foreign policy: realism or idealism? Why?

8. What does the author mean by referencing "the court of public opinion?" Is public opinion important to foreign policy decisions? Why or why not?

Constructing Critical Discourse

Recognizing Inferences

Cultural Note 1   Political leaders often substitute mild and uncontroversial phrases for unpleasant terms so as to please the public. For example, a memo emailed to Pentagon staff members in 2011 noted, "[Obama's] administration prefers to avoid using the term 'Long War' or 'Global War on Terror' [GWOT.] Please use 'Overseas Contingency Operation.'" Thus, it's important to recognize inferences behind diplomatic expressions.

A. Match the words from the Word Bank with their diplomatic equivalents:

Word Bank		
overthrow of a government	torture	civilian casualties
	occupation	bombing

1. The <u>air campaign</u> in the region proved successful in overthrowing the government.

2. There is an ongoing debate in society as to the legality of <u>coercive interrogation</u> of suspects.

3. After declaring war, the country's leaders said they were ready to accept <u>collateral damage</u>.

4. The coalition undertook the <u>liberation</u> of the region.

5. Intervention resulted in <u>regime change</u>.

B. Write a brief news report about a recent instance of intervention covered in the media. In your report, use words and word combinations that reflect diplomatic language.

Forming Hypotheses

A. Study the following quotation from a UN press conference to determine what Kofi Annan requested of the United Nations.

> Kofi Annan, secretary-general of the United Nations from 1997 to 2006, said the following in an April 2000 press conference: "If the UN does not attempt to chart a course for the world's people in the first decades of the new millennium, who will?"

B. Using the pattern shown below for constructing hypotheses, respond to the following questions regarding the question posed by Kofi Annan.

Present condition +	Implications for the present
• If something **happened** now,	• something **would happen**.
• If something **were** true,	• something **would be** true.
• If something **was done** now,	• something **can be done**.

1. Would disbanding the United Nations significantly impact the twenty-first century?
2. Without the United Nations, how would governments coordinate peacekeeping missions?
3. Would any other world power assume the role of the United Nations, or is that already happening even as the United Nations exists today?

Practice Debate

A. Choose one of the roles below and role-play it using at least ten active vocabulary collocations per person.

Situation: A discussion in a UN meeting about possible strategies of dealing with a pending civil war in a particular region.

Role A: A representative of a country advocating intervention.

Role B: A representative of a country opposing intervention.

Role C: A representative of a country involved in the conflict acting in favor of intervention.

Role D: A representative of a country involved in the conflict opposing intervention.

Listening

Pre-Listening

A. Before listening to the audio file, predict the arguments that you'll hear. Fill in the table below.

Foreign governments are justified in interfering in the domestic affairs of sovereign countries.	Foreign governments are not justified in interfering in the domestic affairs of sovereign countries.
•	•
•	•
•	•
•	•
•	•
•	•

While Listening

A. **Listening for general comprehension:** Listen to Audio Recording 2.2 and put a check next to arguments that appear in the table. Write down additional arguments that initially were missing in your table.

B. **Listening for specific details:** Listen to the audio file a second time and evaluate the arguments you listed in the table above as "strong" or "weak." Propose ways of improving the arguments you labeled as "weak."

Post-Listening

A. Which side do you think presented a more persuasive argument? Support your opinion by citing their strongest argument.

B. In every debate, someone has the last word. Predict what the opposing side's response would be to the final argument you heard.

Formatting the Argument: Writing

Wording an Effective Thesis Statement

A persuasive essay begins with a strong thesis statement—a short sentence that expresses the main argument. The rest of the paper supports and develops that statement. A successful thesis meets the following criteria:

1. *A thesis expresses one main idea.* Discussing multiple ideas distracts the reader.
2. *A thesis establishes clear bounds.* Framing the topic prepares the reader for what the essay will cover.
3. *A thesis takes a stand.* Plainly stating one's position helps the reader to follow the logic of subsequent arguments.

A. Read through the following thesis statements and evaluate them on the basis of the criteria listed above. Which are strong? Which are weak? Argue your point.
- Before intervening in another country's domestic affairs, one must consider the cost to civilians and have an effective exit strategy.
- Military intervention is bad.
- Sometimes military intervention is necessary.
- Military intervention can be justified when many civilian lives are at stake.
- There are some positive and negative aspects to intervening in another country's foreign affairs.
- No country should intervene militarily in the affairs of another unless directly threatened by that country.

B. Read the following position paper and identify its thesis statement. Note how the thesis statement guides the rest of the paper.

Interventionism versus Isolationism: Position Paper

The founding documents of the United States emphasize ideals of fairness, justice, and equality. For example, the Declaration of Independence states that "all men are created equal, that they are endowed by their Creator with certain unalienable Rights . . . among these are Life, Liberty and the pursuit of Happiness."[1] However, upholding these ideals occasionally requires intervening in the domestic affairs of other countries. Such an interventionist policy aligns with the maxim that a threat to liberty anywhere is a threat to liberty everywhere. Accordingly, defending human rights at home and abroad at times obligates the United States to intervene in the domestic affairs of other sovereign nations.

Opponents of interventionism argue that intervention by any country violates certain universal principles of respect and political sovereignty. These arguments have as their basis the idea that countries ought to do to others what they would expect others to do to them. However, these arguments fail to see the bigger issue. In 1948 the United Nations drafted and signed the Universal Declaration of Human Rights, which affirmed the "inherent dignity, and the equal and inalienable rights of all members of the human family."[2] It also called on all countries of the United Nations to promote and recognize the same human rights. Therefore, allowing a country to ignore these declared rights not only violates international law, it represents a willful disregard of the obligation that we have to each other as human beings.

This same moral obligation impels us to intervene in the affairs of countries in which international law or human rights are violated. In this way interventionism can reduce crimes against humanity, especially genocide, and deter other countries from violating human rights. As Samantha Power, a Harvard professor focusing on human rights, put it, "stopping the execution of thousands of foreigners [is], in some cases, worth the cost in dollars, troops, and strained alliances."[3] This argument is further supported by the UN's Convention on the Prevention and Punishment of the Crime of Genocide, which requires that a country's sovereignty be breached in order to avoid genocide, an act so repugnant that it has no place in our society. Therefore, intervening in countries that commit crimes against humanity not only saves lives in those countries but also demonstrates a depth of commitment to protecting human rights the world over.

In addition to the aforementioned legal and moral obligations, self-interest can govern the United States' choice of whether or not to intervene. The United States may have an interest in the resolution of a conflict if a country's internal problems begin to affect other allied countries. For example, Somalia has struggled to control its piracy problem, particularly in 2010. After pirates took 1,181 people hostage and private parties and governments spent $238 million on ransoms, the government conceded that circumstances were beyond its control.[4] Not only did these pirates present a threat to Somali citizens, they also presented a threat to anyone traveling in the region, regardless of their citizenship. Consequently, US involvement, along with the deployment of Chinese, Indian, Japanese, and Russian naval forces, was both justified and necessary in order to solve the problem. Had these countries opted not to intervene, Somali pirates very well might continue to control the region, harm innocent people, and unlawfully procure millions of dollars.

    In certain circumstances, intervention in the affairs of a sovereign country can protect human rights and human lives.

While promoting national sovereignty among other nations, the United States also recognizes that circumstances such as the violation of international law and human rights require outside intervention.

Notes

1. US Declaration of Independence, para. 2.
2. UN Universal Declaration of Human Rights, Preamble.
3. Samantha Power, *A Problem from Hell: America and the Age of Genocide* (New York: Harper Perennial, 2002).
4. "Somali Piracy: At Sea," www.economist.com /node/18070160.

C. Draft a thesis statement that states your position on intervention. Exchange thesis statements with a classmate and evaluate each other's work based on the criteria above.

Write Your Own Position Paper

A. Write a paper on the topic "Interventionism versus Isolationism" that consists of five to six paragraphs. Be sure to include active vocabulary collocations from this unit.

Formatting the Argument: Speaking

Implementing Rhetorical Strategies

A. Study the following note:

    Strategy Note 1   In Unit 1, we covered the first of the five debate strategies: conjecture, or "what if" questions. In this unit, we will apply the second strategy, definition questions, to the topic of spreading democracy or breaching sovereignty.

    The definition argument involves clearly understanding and defining the words, phrases, and arguments that can be used to support or reject an idea. Dictionary definitions represent the starting point for this strategy. However, phrases, words, and ideas also can be defined.

B. Review the text, highlighting important words or phrases that you could use to support your side of the debate. For example, if you are arguing that foreign governments are not justified in interfering in domestic affairs of sovereign countries, you may want to concentrate on the definitions of "sovereignty," "intervention," and "territorial integrity," and the underlying concepts that are related to these definitions.

List five important words or phrases with definitions that support your side of the argument.

1. _____
2. _____
3. _____
4. _____
5. _____

C. During the debate, you can use these definitions to support your argument or to weaken the argument of the other side. For instance, you could ask and answer something like, "If we agree that 'sovereignty' means 'a nation having total authority over a geographical area,' how can one nation legitimately attack another?"

Based on the definitions you have listed above, write five sentences or questions you could use in your debate.

1. _____
2. _____
3. _____
4. _____
5. _____

D. As you prepare for the debate, you can predict that the other side will use definitions to support their argument. You can argue against these definitions by pointing out weaknesses in the definitions. To illustrate, the other side may argue that intervention is justified based on a definition of "morality." You could argue that it's the responsibility of the citizens of a particular nation to define morality, so one nation's morality is not the same as another nation's morality.

Review the text and list five key words or phrases with their definitions that the other side could use in their side of the debate. Then list how you would argue against these definitions.

1. _____
2. _____
3. _____
4. _____
5. _____

E. Review and application of previous debate strategies:

In Unit 1, we covered the first of the five debate strategies: conjecture. In preparation for the debate, apply this strategy to support your argument or weaken the argument of the other side.

Framing Templates

A. The following expressions can be used to **express disagreement**. Review these framing templates and incorporate them into both your oral and written arguments.

1. Although I can agree with X on . . . , I cannot accept their assumption/claim/ . . . that . . .
2. The argument that . . . seems weak because . . .
3. On the one hand, I agree that . . . On the other hand, I'm not sure if . . .
4. Anyone familiar with . . . should disagree that . . .
5. The claim that . . . can be proved wrong by addressing . . .

Dealing with Questions

A. There may be times during the debate when you do not fully understand a question. Use the following **clarifying questions** in case this situation arises.

- Did I understand correctly that you are asking about X?
- Would you like for me to address X or Y?
- I am afraid I did not quite understand the question. Could you clarify what you mean?
- Are you interested in X?
- What do you mean by X?
- Could you rephrase the question? I am not sure what you mean.

Speaking

A. Oral Presentation: Prepare a three- to five-minute oral presentation arguing your position. After practicing, record your presentation and then listen to it. What areas do you need to improve on? Be prepared to give your presentation in class.

B. Debate: Now it's time for you to debate. Synthesize all your notes dealing with arguments, useful active vocabulary collocations, and framing templates to assist you during the actual debate. Remember that these will serve as a reference only, not as a text to be read directly during your debate.

Reflection

Self-evaluation

A. Think back over the work you have done thus far. Plot your responses to the following statements on the scale.
1. I felt prepared to debate this topic.
2. I was motivated to debate this topic.
3. I put a lot of effort into preparing to debate this topic.

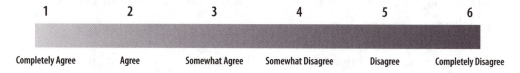

1	2	3	4	5	6
Completely Agree	Agree	Somewhat Agree	Somewhat Disagree	Disagree	Completely Disagree

B. If most of your answers were at the right end of the spectrum, what can you do to move to the left end? If most of your answers were at the left end of the spectrum, what can you do to stay in that area?

Vocabulary Recall

Identify **ten** active vocabulary collocations you have learned and used in this chapter that you feel were most beneficial to you as you debated.

1. _____
2. _____
3. _____
4. _____
5. _____
6. _____
7. _____
8. _____
9. _____
10. _____

UNIT
3

Wealth Redistribution versus Self-Reliance

Mind the Gap

(Credit: Ed Yourdon from New York City, New York)

Pre-Reading

Introducing the Issue

A. Outside of class, interview three nonnative and (if possible) native English speakers. Record their answers to the questions below.

    1. Does your home country have a large gap between the rich and poor?

    2. To what extent do you think quality of life differs between the rich and the poor?

    3. Which countries do you think have the widest and narrowest gaps between the rich and poor?

B. Use the following map of wealth distribution to locate the countries mentioned in your interviews and either confirm or reject your hypotheses.

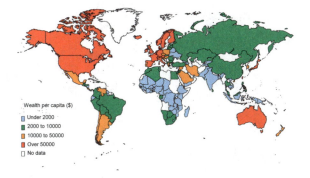

(Credit: This map is a reproduction of a map created by UNU-WIDER, which commissioned the original research for the map and holds copyright thereon. Used by permission of UNU-WIDER.)

C. Now, get into groups and present the results of your survey to a few of your classmates. In this mini presentation, be sure to address the questions below and also create two questions of your own to generate a group discussion.

1. How accurate were your participants' opinions based on the map?
2. Did you find mostly similar or differing responses?
3. What factors might contribute to participants' assumptions?
4. _____
5. _____

D. Study **Language Note 1** on the meaning of "wealth redistribution" and "self-reliance." Explain to your partner which of the two concepts is closer to your personal views and why.

Language Note 1

| **WEALTH DISTRIBUTION** is based on the idea of the transfer of income, wealth, or property from certain individuals to others that is carried out by means of social mechanisms, such as taxation, monetary policies, welfare, nationalization, charity, and the like. Most often it refers to progressive redistribution, from the rich to the poor, although it also may refer to regressive redistribution, from the poor to the rich. | **SELF-RELIANCE** is the capacity to manage one's own affairs, make one's own judgments, and provide for oneself. The concept of self-reliance focuses on the effort of individuals to provide for themselves instead of seeking institutional support. |

E. Analyze the title "Mind the Gap." Look at the pictures below and explain possible uses
    of the expression "mind the gap."

    1. _____
    2. _____
    3. _____
    4. _____
    5. _____

(Credit: By Juergen Rosskamp)

(Credit: By Joe Knapp)

F. Based on the title "Mind the Gap," make a list of issues that might appear in the article.

    1. helping the poor
    2. _____
    3. _____
    4. _____
    5. _____

Creating Mind Maps

A. Brainstorm as many words as you know associated with the challenges a country might face in its spheres of public and private responsibilities. Arrange your ideas to create two separate mind maps according to the pattern shown below. After reading the article, you will be able to add more information, so leaving boxes blank at this point is okay.

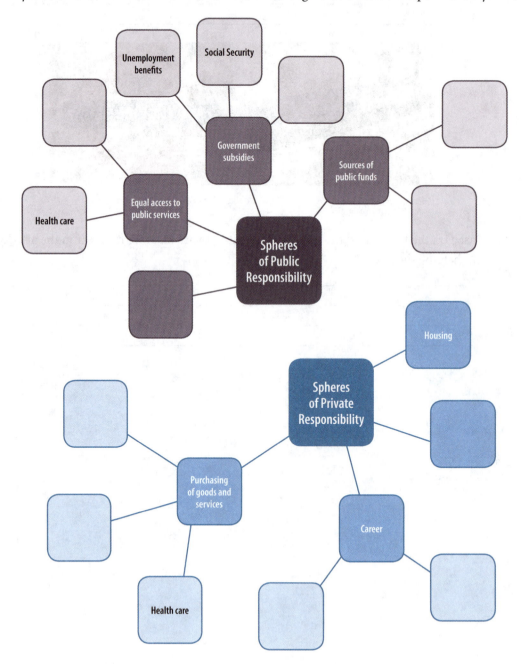

B. Compare your maps with those of your classmates to generate additional ideas. After completing each of the two maps, decide which topic areas can help bridge the gap between the two maps. In other words, which issues concerning public and private spheres of responsibility intersect?

Discussing Facts and Opinions

A. Complete the quotation below with the following words: *character, prosperity, themselves, class, wage, poor, strong.*

> You cannot help the (1) _____ by destroying the rich. You cannot strengthen the weak by weakening the (2) _____. You cannot bring about (3) _____ by discouraging thrift. You cannot lift the wage earner up by pulling the (4) _____ payer down. You cannot further the brotherhood of man by inciting (5) _____ hatred. You cannot build (6) _____ and courage by taking away people's initiative and independence. You cannot help people permanently by doing for them what they could and should do for (7) _____.
>
> Abraham Lincoln

B. Summarize Abraham Lincoln's position. Do you agree with his views on wealth redistribution? Brainstorm specific reasons that support your opinion, then share them with a partner.

Studying the Topic

Focused Reading

A. As you read "Mind the Gap," list the arguments for both sides of the debate in the following table.

Wealth Redistribution	Self-Reliance
•	•
•	•
•	•
•	•
•	•
•	•
•	•
•	•
•	•

B. 🎧 Check your pronunciation of unfamiliar words from the text as you listen to Audio Recording 3.1.

Mind the Gap
Brooke Ward

According to the United Nations University World Institute for Development Economics Research, a massive 85 percent of global household wealth is held by just one-tenth of the world's population. The data also show that the gap between the rich and poor has continually expanded in recent decades, both within and between countries.[1] While the greatest discrepancies are found in such highly developed nations as the United Kingdom and the United States, economic disparity exists everywhere in the world. For example, income inequality has surged in the world's most highly populated areas, including India and China.[2]

The World Economic Forum (WEF) suggests that these gaps threaten economic and social stability, thus adding fuel to the fire of current geopolitical conflicts. "If we do not deal with economic disparity we will have more problems dealing with other risks," asserted Kristel Van der Elst, co-editor of WEF's 2011 Global Risks Report. She suggested that wealth imbalance could be connected to crime and terrorism, a lack of food security, wide-scale health concerns, and even government failure. A case in point is the late 2010 and early 2011 Tunisian and Egyptian revolutions. Corruption and freedom of speech were factors at play in both instances of rebellion, but the people ultimately were driven to action by economic inequality. They wanted to see prosperity across the board but felt spurned by corrupt administrations that profited off their citizens.[3]

Presently, Scandinavian countries tend to have the smallest gap between the rich and poor, as measured by the Gini index. This is the most commonly used measurement of household income distribution, in which a lower coefficient represents a more equal distribution. For instance, in 2010 Sweden had the lowest Gini coefficient in the world at 23, while the highest was Namibia at 70.[4]

Worldwide, governments have attempted to close the gap and boost living standards for their poor through the principle of wealth redistribution. In Sweden, for example, government services include equal access to health care and dental subsidies. The country also has a long tradition of using tax revenue to provide postsecondary education free of charge to its citizens.[5]

When discussing the term "wealth redistribution," it is important to note that what is actually being shuffled around is money income rather than preexisting physical and financial assets, land, or resources.[6] Most democratic countries have some form of wealth redistribution, often fed by a progressive income tax system by which those who earn higher incomes are taxed at a higher rate. All public services, including such basics as road maintenance, garbage collection, and emergency response crews, rely on some form of wealth redistribution. Often, such services are seen as a given since they benefit all members of a community. Other services, specifically social "safety nets" that support those of a lower socioeconomic status, are controversial because tax money is collected from the general population to fund programs that benefit a specific sector of society. Understandably, the concept lends itself to a heated debate on both moral and economic grounds.

On the one hand, there are those who say it's the government's job to redistribute wealth in order to provide equal access to services such as education and health care and to maintain a certain standard of living. Doing so, they argue, is socially just because wealthy people earn their fortunes on the backs of the working class. As such, rich people have a moral obligation to help the poor.

This argument rests on the belief that lower-class individuals are exploited through unfair wages and poor working conditions, and are held back from career advancement and other opportunities owing to a lack of education. Those who share this opinion believe that education is a foundation for a successful life and a means of improving individual circumstances.

Others subscribe to this belief because of their personal religious convictions regarding charity. Some Christians, for instance, cite Jesus's example as an advocate for sharing one's substance and caring for the downtrodden and needy. For them, taking care of society's needy is a faith-driven responsibility.

Then there are the practical arguments. For example, when wealth stratifications are less extreme, there is a larger middle class with a higher overall standard of living, and thus a higher purchasing power. A higher volume of consumers translates into greater cash flow. Financial inequality and the associated disadvantages and social problems also impact significantly on crime rates. Many studies have established a correlation between poverty and crime, particularly violent crime. For example, one study concluded that the lower per capita rate of homicide in Canada has a proportional relationship to smaller income differences than what was observed in the United States.

Researchers suggest that raising the standard of living among the poor will reduce the level of violent crime.[7]

On the other hand, there is the belief that governments do not have a right to redistribute wealth, in part because the services they are funding should not even be a function of government. Critics of government-funded programs advocate privatization of everything from pre-schools to prisons, arguing that such programs are nowhere near as efficient and are exponentially more expensive than what the private sector can offer.

This group favors limited government intervention and tends to see redistribution as a type of handout that encourages laziness, to the detriment of those who work to earn their living. Social supports, such as welfare, misplace funds that otherwise could benefit a greater portion of the population and are counterproductive to society as a whole because they provide an incentive for lower-income individuals to live on the dole.

What's more is that these subsidies take the burden of responsibility off individuals. There are cases involving people who genuinely need help getting by, including those with injuries and disabilities that prevent them from working, or those affected by economic crises who find themselves temporarily out of work. Unfortunately, those needs go largely unmet, owing to a public that thinks it's the government's job to care for others. From this perspective, institutionalized welfare programs discourage voluntary charitable giving.

At their most extreme, those who are opposed to government-mandated wealth redistribution consider it blatant theft.[8] Poor people have no claim on those who work to earn their money, they say. America, for example, is a nation that values economic self-reliance rooted in a strong work ethic. There are those who believe that too many people abuse the system and cheat taxpayers out of their hard-earned money simply because they are unwilling to work themselves.

Early American capitalism was founded on the principle of laissez-faire economics whereby private individuals and organizations could conduct business without government intervention in the form of taxes and other regulations. However, with a growing population and increased social demands, the system could not sustain itself. In 1861 the first income tax was assessed to help pay for the Civil War. In 1935 social security was established, followed just a few years later with Roosevelt's implementation of a progressive income tax system that continues to serve as the basic model today.[9]

Over time the issue of wealth redistribution has become a distinguishing feature of two US political parties. Democrats, for example, are more than twice as likely to advocate in favor of redistribution.[10]

This was demonstrated by President Barak Obama's universal health care reforms that followed several failed attempts by predecessors.

In 2008 roughly half of all American citizens were in favor of progressive taxation, and two in three believed that those in higher income brackets paid too little in taxes. This finding reflects the fact that most Americans see themselves as members of the middle class, even if they belong to other socioeconomic strata.[11]

Despite the economic hierarchy that exists in the United States, public belief in the American dream persists. Realistically, the poorest 5 percent of Americans are still wealthier than 70 percent of the rest of the global population.[12] Regardless of however removed the haves may be from the have-nots, the notion of progress saves the United States from the same far-reaching, bottom-up rebellion witnessed in Tunisia and Egypt. Yet, if the WEF is accurate in its prediction, more upheaval can be expected around the globe as the world's underprivileged and even downright destitute become tired of being taken advantage of. Are they correct in assuming that the surest way to avoid future hostility is by governments mandating wealth redistribution?

Notes

1. "Personal Assets from a Global Perspective," United Nations University—World Institute for Development Economics Research, accessed October 22, 2013, www.wider.unu.edu/.

2. Dan Wesley, "Income Distribution by Country," *Visual Economics*, accessed October 22, 2013, www.visualeconomics.com/income-distribution-by-country/.

3. Kristel Van der Elst and Nicholas Davis, eds., *Global Risks 2011*, 6th ed. (Geneva: World Economic Forum, 2011).

4. "Measuring Inequality in Household Income: The Gini Coefficient," UK Statistics Authority, accessed October 22, 2013, www.statistics.gov .uk.

5. "Policy Areas," Government Offices of Sweden, accessed October 22, 2013, www.government.se /sb/d/2093.

6. "Redistribution," Stanford Encyclopedia of Philosophy, last modified June 21, 2011, http:// plato.stanford.edu/entries/redistribution/.

7. M. Daly, M. Wilson, and S. Vasdev, "Income Inequality and Homicide Rates in Canada and the United States," *Canadian Journal of Criminology* 43 (2001): 219–36.

8. Anthony Flood, "'Redistribution' as Euphemism or, Who Owns What?," *Philosophy Pathways* 65 (August 24, 2003), www.philosophypathways .com/newsletter/issue68.html.

9. Andrew Achenbaum, *Social Security Visions and Revisions* (New York: Cambridge University Press, 1986).

10. Frank Newport, Jeffrey M. Jones, Lydia Saad, Alec M. Gallup, and Fred L. Israel, *Winning the White House: The Gallup Poll* (New York: Checkmark Books, 2009).

11. Ibid.

12. Branko Milanovic, *The Haves and Have Nots* (New York: Basic Books, 2010).

Checking Comprehension

A. Select the most appropriate answer to each question.

    1. The main purpose of this article is to _____.

        a. discuss economic problems faced by many developing nations.

        b. argue in favor of minimizing the levels of income inequality.

        c. present arguments both for and against wealth redistribution.

        d. explain how the gap between the rich and poor has widened.

    2. Which sentence below fits best at the end of the third paragraph?

        a. Many countries experiencing economic tumult would do well to pattern their wealth-redistribution programs after those in Sweden.

        b. Not all countries have a large percentage of citizens demanding wealth redistribution.

        c. Economic instability in the European Union has caused many Scandinavians to seek government aid.

        d. The United States' Gini coefficient of 45 implies that the country's wealth is distributed quite evenly.

    3. What is actually being rearranged when we discuss wealth redistribution?

        a. Financial income

        b. Natural resources

        c. Preexisting assets

        d. Private property

4. According to the article, how does Jesus's example relate to this debate?
   a. He was content despite his poverty.
   b. He paid taxes like everyone else.
   c. He cared for the less fortunate.
   d. He told the wealthy to give to the poor.

5. "Democrats are more than twice as likely to advocate in favor of wealth redistribution." Based on this passage from the text, one can infer that those in favor of _____ are Democrats.
   a. applying progressive income taxes
   b. privatizing schools and prisons
   c. reorganizing social classes
   d. minimizing the middle class

6. In 2008 two in three Americans believed that those in higher income brackets paid too little in taxes, therefore one can infer that _____.
   a. lower income brackets aren't paying enough taxes.
   b. most Americans don't consider themselves wealthy.
   c. the United States has fixed income tax rates.
   d. America should reduce its debt by increasing taxes.

7. The main idea of the last paragraph is that _____.
   a. Americans are wealthy enough that they likely will not have to worry about revolutions in the near future.
   b. if governments don't distribute the wealth evenly among citizens, the world can expect rebellions to continue.
   c. citizens' hopes and dreams prevent the United States from facing a fate similar to that of less stable countries.
   d. social hierarchies are just one of the factors that cause instability in the public and private sectors.

Mastering Vocabulary

Active Vocabulary Collocations	
Government and Society	**General**
1. economic discrepancy/disparity/inequality	1. a case in point
2. fair wages and safe working conditions	2. a heated debate
3. government subsidies	3. at one's most extreme
4. progressive income tax system	4. factors at play
5. public services	5. free of charge
6. safety net	6. the most commonly used
7. social class/strata	7. to add fuel to
8. socially just	8. to be driven to action
9. to earn one's fortunes	9. to be nowhere near
10. to live on the dole	10. to deal with the problem
11. to provide equal opportunities	11. to establish a relationship
12. to raise the standard of living	12. to have a moral obligation
13. to tax at a higher rate	13. to provide an incentive for
14. universal health care	14. to see as a given
15. wealth redistribution	15. to subscribe to the belief that
16. to spread democracy	16. to take something into account

Expanding Vocabulary

A. Complete the mind maps begun in the pre-reading section by using active vocabulary collocations above. In order to do this, you may need to expand your mind maps by adding new boxes and connections.

B. Find terms in the Government and Society column of the active vocabulary collocations that match with definitions below.
1. The transfer of income, wealth, or property from certain individuals to others that is carried out by means of social mechanisms, such as taxation, monetary policies, welfare, nationalization, charity, and the like.
2. Wealth and income differences among individuals and groups within a society.
3. Providing all members of a society with medical coverage at the expense of the government.
4. A working environment free of health hazards.
5. Safeguards put in place against possible misfortune or difficulty.
6. A society in which people have the ability to realize their potential.
7. Treating employees and others without discrimination, especially gender, race, or age.
8. Government services provided to all citizens of a country.
9. Government assistance for businesses.
10. A tax that takes a larger percentage from high-income individuals than from low-income individuals.

C. In numbers 1–5 below, cross out the item that doesn't fit and explain to a partner the connection between the remaining words.
1. wages, incentive, social strata, fortunes
2. health care, education, taxes, welfare
3. fund, safety net, tax rates, subsidize
4. hierarchy, social justice, moral obligation, charity
5. stable, living on the dole, self-sufficient, career

D. ⊕ Go to COCA (http://corpus.byu.edu/coca/). Click on COLLOCATES and type "[v*]" in the box that appears. Under SORTING AND LIMITS find the dropdown menu next to MINIMUM and select MUTUAL INFO. For each question below, type the bolded words in the WORD(S) box and click SEARCH. Select the appropriate verbs for each blank using the top twelve collocations as the Word Bank for each item.

1. Although the company _____ to _____ **fair wages**, the workers are _____ for higher salaries.

2. Many citizens are _____ in a **heated debate**, which was _____ by the mention of canceling welfare programs.

3. In order to _____ _____ important **public services**, the hospital will need to _____ on donations.

4. The United States cannot _____ a **safety net** for the world and must _____ itself from becoming a global welfare magnet.

5. Married couples generally _____ a higher **standard of living**; however, it becomes difficult to _____ and will likely _____ when children come.

E. Write five sentences that you could use in the debate to support your stance. In each sentence, use one of the bolded words above with at least one of its collocations.

Exploring the Meaning

A. Write out as many active vocabulary collocations as possible that can be used while talking about (1) government, (2) the rich, and (3) the poor. Some collocations might fall into multiple categories.

Government	The Rich	The Poor
•	•	•
•	•	•
•	•	•
•	•	•
•	•	•
•	•	•
•	•	•

B. Scan the article to find mention of Sweden, the United Kingdom, Namibia, Egypt, and Canada. With a partner, use the collocations from the previous activity to answer the questions below for each country.

1. Does this country have an equal distribution of wealth?
2. What factors likely led to this distribution?
3. What have been the effects of this distribution on citizens?
4. What advice would you give to the president of your home country based on this country's example?

C. Match the expressions in the left column with their equivalents in the right column.

1.	a case in point	a.	to foster
2.	a heated debate	b.	to agree that
3.	to provide an incentive for	c.	to tackle an issue
4.	commonly used	d.	a good example of
5.	to subscribe to the belief that	e.	a vigorous discussion
6.	to deal with a problem	f.	widely spread

D. Finish the sentences below using the most appropriate of the two collocations in parentheses.

1. Proponents of big government believe that . . . (to have a moral obligation/ safety net)

   _____.

2. Wealth redistribution can lead to a situation in which . . . (at one's most extreme/ to live on the dole)

   _____.

3. Cuts in public spending during the economic crisis . . . (to add fuel/to be driven to action)

   _____.

4. Advocates of self-reliance highlight the role of the individual in . . . (to earn one's fortunes/factors at play)

   _____

5. The affluent disagree that . . . (socially just/to tax at a higher rate)

   _____

E. Match each quotation below from prominent US political figures with its main idea, and write out at least two related collocations from the active vocabulary list that support each opinion.

Our new Constitution is now established, and has an appearance that promises permanency; but in this world nothing can be said to be certain, except death and taxes.

Benjamin Franklin

The democracy will cease to exist when you take away from those who are willing to work and give to those who would not.

Thomas Jefferson

The wisdom of man never yet contrived a system of taxation that would operate with perfect equality.

Andrew Jackson

Taxes, after all, are dues that we pay for the privileges of membership in an organized society.

Franklin D. Roosevelt

Collecting more taxes than is absolutely necessary is legalized robbery.

Calvin Coolidge

Main Idea	Collocations
1. Taxes are necessary	Safety net, public services, free of charge
2. Taxes are beneficial	
3. It is important to limit taxes	
4. Self-reliance is important	
5. Taxation likely doesn't lead to social justice	

F. Which of the five politicians above do you agree with most? Explain your reasoning.

G. Study the figure below that illustrates tax rates in various countries. Choose a country from those cited and explain whether you think its tax rate contributes to the standard of living of its citizens based on your knowledge of that country's economic situation, level of economic disparity, amount and quality of public services, and any other background information that may be relevant. Use at least five vocabulary words or phrases in your answer.

	Mean Income Tax Rates as a % of Personal Income[a]		Mean Income Tax Rates as a % of Personal Income[a]
Korea	17	Netherlands	38.25
Mexico	18	Greece	38.50
New Zealand	21	Spain	39
Ireland	26	Denmark	42
Japan	27	Turkey	43
Australia	28	Poland	44
Iceland	29	Czech Republic	44.25
United States	29	Finland	44.50
Switzerland	29.50	Italy	45
Canada	32	Austria	46
United Kingdom	34	Sweden	47
Luxembourg	35	Hungary	49
Portugal	36	France	50
Norway	37	Germany	52
Slovak Republic	38	Belgium	55

[a]Based on OECD 2005 data

Discussing the Article

A. Working with a partner, use active vocabulary collocations to answer the following questions based on the text.
    1. What do UN statistics on economic disparity in the world indicate? What inferences can be made from the data given in the article?
    2. What consequences does economic inequality have on developing countries, on the one hand, and on developed ones, on the other?

3. In your opinion, what factors could contribute to the low Gini coefficients found in Scandinavian countries? Why is the coefficient so high in countries like Namibia?

4. Does wealth redistribution bridge the gap between social classes? If yes, how? If no, why not?

5. What moral issues does wealth redistribution raise? Do wealthy individuals have a moral obligation to help the poor? Why or why not?

6. What are the advantages to government-run social programs? What are the advantages to leaving such programs to the private sector?

7. In what ways does the upper class exploit the lower class? In what ways does the upper class support the lower class?

8. Why does the author include a paragraph about religious conviction in relation to social justice and welfare?

9. Is there a link between the welfare state and the "burden of responsibility" placed on individuals? If so, what evidence supports this link? What evidence fails to support it?

10. What is an alternative to progressive tax systems? Explain the advantages and disadvantages of both.

Constructing Critical Discourse

Recognizing Inferences

A. Match the words and word combinations in the Word Bank with their diplomatic equivalents underlined in each sentence.

Word Bank		
cuts in social programs	to fire employees	the poor
economic crisis	the elderly	a recession

1. The newly elected administration undertook a number of <u>welfare reforms</u> in order to stabilize the economy.

2. The economy in the region can still be characterized by <u>negative growth</u> in spite of measures taken to fight the credit crunch.

3. The city has a large percentage of <u>underprivileged</u> mostly residing in economically depressed neighborhoods.

4. State legislators discussed a proposal to require a special driver's test for <u>senior citizens</u> in order to avoid health-related road accidents.
5. Cuts in government subsidies to small businesses led to many companies having to <u>downsize</u>.

Forming Hypotheses

A. Study the following case to determine the difference between perceived and actual effects of a luxury tax.

> In the 1990s, during the presidency of George H. W. Bush, the government introduced the so-called luxury tax on the purchase of luxury commodities such as yachts, deluxe cars, and the like. However, taxing the elite did not bring the anticipated results as the tax revenues proved insignificant. Ironically, the tax mainly hit the middle class in the form of lost jobs in related businesses, such as yacht maintenance, jewelry, and fur retail. A couple of years later, the tax was annulled. In spite of the negative fallout associated with implementing such a tax in America, many countries continually toy with the idea of levying a luxury tax.

B. Using the pattern shown below for constructing hypotheses, respond to the following question regarding luxury taxes.

Past conditional	+	Implications for the past
• If somebody **had known** in the past, • If something **had been** true in the past, • If something **had been done** in the past,	→	• something **would have happened** then. • something else **would have been** true then. • something else **could have been done** then.

Has the country in which you live or were born ever tried to impose a luxury tax?
1. If yes, what consequences did the introduction of such a tax have? Speculate on the following hypothetical scenario: Had the government known in advance the consequences of such a tax, would it have acted differently?
2. If no, what effects would such a tax have brought about by now had it been introduced in your country a year ago?

Practice Debate

A. Choose one of the roles below and role-play it using at least ten active vocabulary collocations per person.

Situation: A presidential candidate is holding a meeting with his electorate in a crucial metropolitan city. Citizens in attendance vary from wealthy business executives to underprivileged residents.

Role A: The presidential candidate trying to balance out the interests of the affluent and the underprivileged classes.

Role B: The presidential running mate.

Role C: Representatives from underprivileged groups of society.

Role D: Representatives from the middle class.

Role E: Representatives from the wealthy sector of society.

Listening

Pre-Listening

A. Before listening to the audio file, predict the arguments that you'll hear. Fill in the table below.

Governments should mandate wealth redistribution.	Governments should encourage self-reliance.
•	•
•	•
•	•
•	•
•	•
•	•

🎧 While Listening

A. **Listening for general comprehension:** Listen to Audio Recording 3.2 and put a check next to arguments that appear in the table. Write down additional arguments that initially were missing in your table.

B. **Listening for specific details:** Listen to the audio file a second time and evaluate the arguments you listed in the table above as "strong" or "weak." Propose ways of improving the arguments you labeled as "weak."

Post-Listening

A. Which side do you think presented a more persuasive argument? Support your opinion by citing their strongest argument.

B. In every debate, someone has the last word. Predict what the opposing side's response would be to the final argument you heard.

Formatting the Argument: Writing

Outlining

In addition to having valid arguments to support your thesis, your essay should be structured in such a way that the reader can follow your train of thought. Below are some guidelines for structuring your essay.

1. Introduction: A persuasive essay begins with an introductory paragraph that outlines the issues and states your thesis.
2. Main Body: The main body of the essay consists of three to four paragraphs that set forth your key arguments and supporting evidence aimed at establishing the thesis. Avoid unsupported assertions and provide solid data to strengthen your argument. By addressing opposing points of view, you anticipate doubts and objections that a reader might have. A successful counterargument begins with a point of concession, introduced with a phrase like *Some might object . . . , It might seem that . . . ,* or *Admittedly . . . ,* followed by the opposing viewpoint stated as briefly and clearly as possible. The counterargument typically goes just after the introduction or before the conclusion.
3. A persuasive essay ends with a conclusion that contains a summary of your argument and restates your thesis statement.

A. Read the essay below and arrange the key points in the following outline.

Thesis statement

Counterargument

Argument 1

    Evidence 1

Argument 2

    Evidence 2

Argument 3

    Evidence 3

Conclusion (Restatement of thesis)

Wealth Redistribution versus Self-Reliance: Position Paper

Across the globe great discrepancies exist between the rich and the poor. The United Nations found that 85 percent of the wealth is held by only one-tenth of the world's population.[1] Such disparity exists across the world, but the greatest differences occur in highly developed nations, such as the United States. Wealth disparity leads to a variety of problems within society, and if the wealth gap continues to grow, then economic and social stability will be threatened. Because of these problems, the government should redistribute the wealth of its citizens.

Some people argue that overtaxation of the wealthy creates a disincentive for them to generate more wealth, which ends up hurting the economy. Further, people argue that if the poor receive government handouts and subsidies, they will be incentivized to live on the dole and not earn a living wage. The idea is that people should provide for themselves and that the economy will cease to function if the government takes from people who are willing to work in order to give to those who are not willing to work. However, many poor people and rich people were born to their situations and misfortunes, and a lack of opportunities often stifles otherwise hard-working, productive individuals.

Wealth redistribution would benefit individuals because those in lower social classes often suffer from fewer opportunities and other misfortunes. They frequently lack the means to better their education and pursue opportunities to improve their situation. Studies have also suggested that wealth imbalance could be connected to crime. For example, one study estimated that much of the variation in homicide rates in different states could be accounted for by differences in the amount of inequality in each state.[2] Furthermore, studies have found that individual health correlates with one's economic status. A study conducted over the span of thirty-three years found that social class has a powerful influence on whether people grow up healthy or beset by illnesses, including general sickness, respiratory problems, and psychological distress in both men and women.[3] As individuals in the lower social classes suffer from fewer educational opportunities, more crime, and poorer health, wealth redistribution would benefit them.

Wealth redistribution would also benefit a nation as a whole. Studies have shown that a vibrant middle class benefits a nation. When a nation has a strong middle class, it creates an overall higher standard of living that allows for greater purchasing power and cash flow. Further, giving the middle class more purchasing power will help spur growth to the benefit of all.[4] For example, a study conducted by the International Monetary Fund found that greater income equality positively correlated with stronger economic growth.[5] The study cited modern and historical examples of inequality and corresponding economic instability, including a comparison of the United States during the 1920s and recent decades. Both time periods witnessed an economic boom accompanied by an increase in inequality and followed by a huge financial crisis.[6] The study concluded that equality appears to

be an important ingredient in promoting and sustaining growth and efficiency.

Because wealth redistribution would benefit both individuals and a nation as a whole, the government should redistribute the wealth to decrease the gap between the rich and the poor. This does not mean that the government should simply take money from one group of people and hand it to another. One way to redistribute wealth is to reevaluate progressive income taxes and ask the wealthy to fulfill their moral obligation to lighten the burden on the underprivileged. While they rarely admit it, the wealthy take for granted that taxes are required of all members of society for the privileges they receive. Governments provide services to everyone, but the wealthiest Americans are the main beneficiaries of things like property rights, zoning rules, patent and copyright provisions, trade pacts, antitrust legislation, and contract regulations.[7]

As the gap between the rich and poor grows wider, the economy will suffer. Because wealth disparity contributes to a variety of problems for individuals and nations, the government should redistribute wealth to raise the standard of living of the poor and middle class.

Notes

1. "Personal Assets from a Global Perspective," United Nations University—World Institute for Development Economics Research.
2. Martin Daly, Margo Wilson, and Shawn Vasdev, "Income Inequality and Homicide Rates in Canada and the United States," *Canadian Journal of Criminology* 43, no. 2 (April 2001): 219–36.

3. "Health: Lower Classes Born to Life of Poorer Health," *Independent*, November 29, 1997, www.independent.co.uk/news/health-lower-classes-born-to-life-of-poorer-health-1296824.html.
4. Ibid., and Robert B. Reich, "(Purchasing) Power to the (Middle Class)," *Wall Street Journal*, June 18, 2011, http://online.wsj.com/article/SB10001424052702304319804576389661050976264.html.

5. Andrew G. Berg and Jonathan D. Ostry, "Equality and Efficiency," *Finance and Development* 48, no. 3 (September 2011): 12–15, www.imf.org/external/pubs/ft/fandd/2011/09/Berg.htm.

6. Ibid.

7. Paul Buchheit and Veronique de Rugy, "The Rich Get More from Government Than Anyone," edited by Jeffery J. Smith, *Progress Report*, accessed October 22, 2013, www.progress.org/2012/catostud.htm.

B. Read the following two paragraphs in support of wealth redistribution. Which paragraph offers solid data to support the author's opinion and which paragraph presents unsupported assertions?

> Since 1980 the distribution of wealth in the United States has changed dramatically. The rich have gotten richer and the poor have gotten poorer. Data from the Economic Policy Institute (EPI), in its "The State of Working America" report, demonstrate that between 1983 and 2010 the top 5 percent of income earners increased their share of the pie by 74.2 percent, while the bottom 60 percent watched their share of national income decrease.
>
> In contrast to the last thirty-two years of increasing inequality, between 1935 and 1975 equality increased in the United States. This did not mean that the rich suffered; it just meant that they increased their wealth in equal proportion to the rest of the country. A number of government policies helped create a more level playing field. During those years the United States had a sharply progressive income tax, and the government spent its money in ways that sustained a strong middle class. It built and maintained the world's best infrastructure and paid its workers union wages. The country created and staffed the world's greatest and most extensive higher-education system and then dramatically subsidized the education of millions of people with low or free tuition and a generous G.I. Bill.

Write Your Own Position Paper

A. Write a position paper on the topic "Wealth Redistribution versus Self-Reliance" that consists of five to six paragraphs. Be sure to include active vocabulary from this unit.

Formatting the Argument: Speaking

Implementing Rhetorical Strategies

A. Study the following note:

> **Strategy Note 1**   In Unit 1, we covered the first of the five debate strategies, conjecture, or "what if" questions, and in Unit 2 we covered definition strategies. In this unit, we focus on the third strategy: issues regarding cause and effect. This is where we include the relationship between something happening and what occurs as a result—cause and consequence, or cause and effect—into our debate preparation.

B. Review the text, highlighting important "cause-and-effect" words or phrases that you could use to support your side of the debate. For example, if you are arguing that it is government's responsibility to redistribute wealth, you could highlight words, phrases, and larger ideas in the text that examine the consequence to a society of a government that fails to care for its poor.

   List five important cause-and-effect relationships that support your side of the argument.

   1. _____
   2. _____
   3. _____
   4. _____
   5. _____

C. During the debate, you can use these cause-and-effect ideas to support your argument or to weaken the argument of the other side. For instance, you could ask and answer something like, "Given a tendency in human nature for laziness, what will happen if governments help the poor too much?"

   Based on the cause-and-effect statements or questions you have listed above, write five sentences or questions you could use in your debate.

   1. _____
   2. _____
   3. _____
   4. _____
   5. _____

D. As you prepare for the debate, you can predict that the other side will use cause-and-effect relationships that support their side of the argument. You can argue against certain consequences by pointing out weaknesses in the cause-and-effect relationship. To illustrate, the other side may argue that wealth redistribution results in the wealthy deciding not to create more wealth because it's too much trouble with little reward since the government is "stealing" their money. You could argue that history has shown that the wealthy need to foster a vibrant middle class in order for the wealthy to remain wealthy.

Review the text and list five key cause-and-effect relationships that the other side could use in their argument. Then list how you would argue against these relationships.

1. _____
2. _____
3. _____
4. _____
5. _____

E. Review and application of previous debate strategies:

In Units 1–2, we covered the first two of the five debate strategies: conjecture and definition. In preparation for the debate, apply these strategies to support your argument or weaken the argument of the other side. Plan ways to use these strategies during the debate.

Framing Templates

A. The following expressions can be used to **address the opposite side**. Review these framing templates and incorporate them into both your oral and written arguments.

1. X apparently assume that . . .
2. In the discussion of X, one controversial issue is . . .
3. On the one hand, X argue that. . . . On the other hand, X claim that . . .
4. While they rarely admit it, X often take for granted that . . .
5. While some are convinced that . . . , others maintain that . . .

Dealing with Questions

A. There may be times during the debate when you **do not have enough information**. Use the following statements in case this situation arises.
- Resolving this issue is going to require conducting additional research.
- I am afraid I do not have the data with me at the moment to provide you with a satisfactory answer.
- I believe we would have to look at specific data, which I am afraid I do not have in front of me at the moment.
- Your question extends beyond my area of expertise, so I am afraid I cannot answer it.

Speaking

A. **Oral Presentation:** Prepare a three- to five-minute oral presentation arguing your position. After practicing, record your presentation and then listen to it. What areas do you need to improve on? Be prepared to give your presentation in class.

B. **Debate:** Now it's time for you to debate. Synthesize all your notes dealing with arguments, useful active vocabulary collocations, and framing templates to assist you during the actual debate. Remember that these will serve as a reference only, not as a text to be read directly during your debate.

Reflection

Self-evaluation

A. Think back over the work you have done thus far. Plot your responses to the following statements on the scale.
  1. I felt prepared to debate this topic.
  2. I was motivated to debate this topic.
  3. I put a lot of effort into preparing to debate this topic.

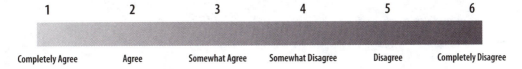

1	2	3	4	5	6
Completely Agree	Agree	Somewhat Agree	Somewhat Disagree	Disagree	Completely Disagree

B. If most of your answers were at the right end of the spectrum, what can you do to move to the left end? If most of your answers were at the left end of the spectrum, what can you do to stay in that area?

Vocabulary Recall

Identify **ten** active vocabulary collocations you have learned and used in this chapter that you feel were most beneficial to you as you debated.

1. _____
2. _____
3. _____
4. _____
5. _____
6. _____
7. _____
8. _____
9. _____
10. _____

UNIT 4

Cultural Preservation versus Diversity

Immigration: Value Added or Value Lost

Pre-Reading

Introducing the Issue

A. Review the figure below of the top ten countries with the highest number of migrants as of 2010. Choose a country from the figure and make a list of possible reasons for the substantial level of migration to and from that country. Share your answers with a partner and identify similar and differing answers.

Country:

Reasons for Ranking:

1. Borders less developed countries
2. _____
3. _____
4. _____
5. _____

Top 10 Countries with the Largest Number of International Migrants (in thousands)	
United States	42,813
Russian Federation	12,270
Germany	10,758
Saudi Arabia	7,289
Canada	7,202
France	6,685
United Kingdom	6,452
Spain	6,378
India	5,436
Ukraine	5,258
World[a]	213,943,812

[a]Top Ten: 52% of the world's total.
Source: United Nations Department of Economic and Social Affairs, Population Division, Trends in International Migrant Stock: The 2008 Revision, UN database (New York: United Nations Department of Economic and Social Affairs, Population Division, 2009). Available at http://esa.un.org/migration/index.asp?panel=1.

B. Study **Cultural Note 1** below regarding the meaning of two metaphors frequently used to describe the fusion of cultures—Melting Pot and Tossed Salad. Explain which of the two concepts reflects the situation in your home country and explain why.

> **Cultural Note 1**
>
> **Melting Pot:** This metaphor is widely used to describe the process of immigrants' assimilation in the United States. According to this metaphor, when mixed together, different nationalities, ethnicities, and cultures create and share a unique identity in their new country of residence.
>
> **Tossed Salad:** This metaphor highlights the ideology of maintaining one's national, ethnic, or cultural identity within a society of the new country of residence.

C. After reading the information in **Language Note 1** below, summarize the title "Immigration: Value Added or Value Lost?" To what aspects of society could immigration add value?

Language Note 1
Value of something such as quality, attitude, or method is its importance or usefulness. If you place a particular value on something, that is the importance or usefulness you think it has. (*Collins Cobuild Dictionary*)
Value Added (in economics) is the amount by which the value of an article is increased at each stage of its production, exclusive of initial costs. (*Oxford American Dictionary*)

D. Make a list of issues that might be discussed in this article based on your analysis of the title.

1. legal framework for immigration

2. _____

3. _____

4. _____

Creating Mind Maps

A. Brainstorm as many words as you know associated with the challenges a country might face in its spheres of cultural identity and immigration-related issues. Arrange your ideas to create two separate mind maps according to the pattern shown below. After reading the article, you will be able to add more information, so leaving boxes blank at this point is okay.

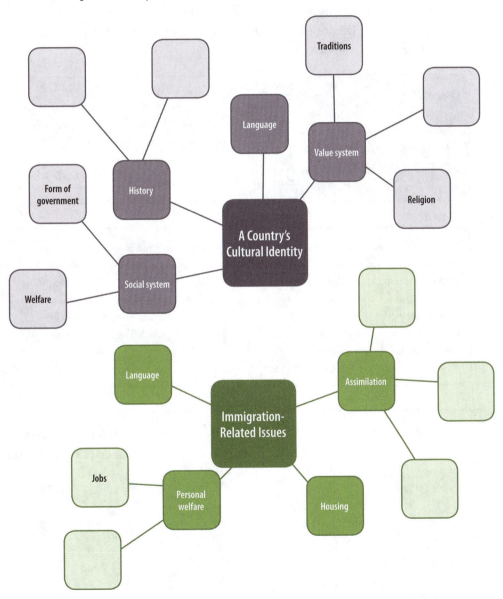

B. Compare your maps with those of your classmates to generate additional ideas. After completing each of the two maps, decide which topic areas can help bridge the gap between the two maps. In other words, which issues concerning a country's cultural identity and immigration-related issues intersect?

Discussing Facts and Opinions

A. After reading the following quotations, fill in the table with benefits of hosting immigrants cited by each US president. Also indicate what you can infer about the core values of America based on these quotations.

> *America was indebted to immigration for her settlement and prosperity. That part of America which had encouraged them most had advanced most rapidly in population, agriculture and the arts.*
>
> *James Madison*

> *The land flourished because it was fed from so many sources—because it was nourished by so many cultures and traditions and peoples.*
>
> *Lyndon B. Johnson*

> *Latinos come to the US to seek the same dreams that have inspired millions of others: they want a better life for their children. . . . Latinos enrich our country with faith in God, a strong ethic of work, community, and responsibility. We can all learn from the strength, solidarity, and values of Latinos.*
>
> *George W. Bush*

> *Now, I strongly believe that we should take on, once and for all, the issue of illegal immigration. . . . Let's stop expelling talented, responsible young people who could be staffing our research labs or starting a new business, who could be further enriching this nation.*
>
> *Barack Obama*

	Benefits of hosting immigrants	Inferences about America's core values
James Madison		
Lyndon B. Johnson		
George W. Bush		
Barack Obama		

Studying the Topic

Focused Reading

A. As you read "Immigration: Value Added or Value Lost," list the arguments for both sides of the debate in the following table.

Cultural Preservation	Diversity through Immigration
•	•
•	•
•	•
•	•
•	•
•	•
•	•
•	•

B. Check your pronunciation of unfamiliar words from the text as you listen to Audio Recording 4.1.

Immigration: Value Added or Value Lost?

Grant Newman

In 1996 two upwardly mobile immigrants from the former Soviet Union started their respective projects in the United States. By 2009 both had amassed enormous wealth to their names. Yet by the end of 2010 each had reaped what he sowed. On the one hand, Sergey Brin, whose family emigrated from Moscow to the United States when he was a boy, became a multi-billionaire thanks to Google, a project that he and a fellow PhD student at Stanford University started in 1996. On the other hand, Armen Kazaryan, an Armenian better known as "Pzo," came to the United States as a refugee in 1996 only to be arrested fourteen years later, in October 2010, in Glendale, California, for masterminding an underground network of doctors that swindled $163 million from Medicare, the United States' public health program for pensioners. These examples highlight the rewards and risks of immigration: Some immigrants readily adopt and emulate their new country's values and norms while others do not—and sometimes at a great price to society. The world as a whole and Americans in particular are left to ponder whether preservation of core cultural values possibly outweighs the cultural diversity brought about by immigration.

Critics of immigration argue that it spells the eventual disruption of a country's founding population, its language, and its culture. They further contend that, in the United States, if enough immigrants fail to develop loyalty to their new country and adopt a common understanding of the political process, then the political structure will break down. No central values will prevail and America will become a mere home away from home where people are more in touch with their native cultures and homelands than with the neighborhoods in which they live. According to Samuel Huntington, a Harvard academic, the high number of Hispanic immigrants actually hinders their assimilation and ultimately stands to "divide the United

States into two peoples, two cultures, and two languages" stemming from a rejection of "Anglo-Protestant values that built the American dream."[1] Lowering the relative number of immigrants by halting their inflow might make assimilation more likely, which in turn would work toward preserving a core language and culture.

Restricting immigration could also have some economic benefit by reserving jobs for native-born citizens. In 2004 America's labor force included 21.4 million immigrants.[2] As cheap labor floods the market, wages for all decrease according to the principles of supply and demand. George Borjas of Harvard University estimates that the wages of native-born workers decrease by about 4 percent for every 10 percent increase in immigrants with similar skills.[3] According to this logic, protectionist policies, including a restriction on immigration, will provide more opportunities and higher wages for native-born laborers and service professionals alike.

Nevertheless, advocates of immigration argue that immigrants neither lower wages nor take away jobs from local members of the population. David Card of the University of California, Berkeley, has found little connection between immigrants and lower wages.[4] Moreover, Gianmarco Ottaviano of the University of Bologna and Giovanni Peri of the University of California, Davis, contend that about 90 percent of native-born Americans actually enjoy higher wages thanks to immigrants, who bring new skills and ideas, spend money, and pay taxes.[5] In this same vein, research by the Pew Hispanic Center suggests that native-born Americans and Hispanic immigrants predominantly work in different industries, thereby implying that immigrants do not take away as many jobs as some may believe.[6]

But immigrants perform more than just backbreaking labor. Highly educated minds increasingly are crossing borders in search of high-paying jobs and environments in which to bring ideas to life. As aforementioned, Mr. Brin cofounded Google. Additionally, Eric Shogren, an entrepreneur from Minnesota who immigrated to Russia in the mid 1990s, founded one of Novosibirsk's most successful restaurant chains. Some Indians, such as Pankaj Ghemawat, are ordained gurus in the American business community while others, such as the late C. K. Prahalad, have already been beatified. Furthermore, Vivek Wadhwa of Harvard Law School reports that "a quarter of America's engineering and technology firms founded between 1995 and 2005 had an immigrant founder."[7] Chinese entrepreneurs are creating jobs in Africa, albeit not without controversy.[8] Thus, immigration advocates claim that immigration actually creates jobs for local populations.

Lastly, immigration can improve a country's demographic situation. Without immigration, Italy's population would have decreased by 75,000 souls in 2009. Thanks to immigration, its population increased by 295,000. Accordingly, "foreign workers fill a hole created by the shrinking of the native population."[9] Immigration can also rejuvenate an aging population.

R. T. Rybak, a former mayor of Minneapolis, Minnesota, boasts that before embracing immigration, his city was "aging, mostly white, and monoglot. Now it has a more international dimension."[10] In the face of a shrinking dependency ratio, immigration can prove to be a fountain of youth for elderly countries.

In the United States, immigration represents an especially thorny issue. With the exception of a dwindling, truly native American Indian population, the United States is a country of immigrants. Appropriately, the United States enacted a liberal immigration policy for about the first century of its formal existence. Between 1830 and 1850, the proportion of foreign-born individuals in the United States jumped from roughly 1.6 percent to 9.7 percent, according to US Census figures. But this "liberal" policy presupposed that immigrants to the United States would Americanize. Theodore Roosevelt, the twenty-sixth US president, stated in 1894: "We welcome the German and the Irishman who becomes an American. We have no use for the German or Irishman who remains such. . . . He must revere only our flag; not only must it come first, but no other flag should even come second."[11]

As a result of increased animosity toward immigrants after World War I, the United States began restricting immigration. As Edward P. Hutchinson, a professor of sociology at the University of Pennsylvania, wrote, "Anti-alien sentiments were aroused, together with fears of allegedly unassimilated foreign-born minorities and 'hyphenated Americans.'"[12] Consequently, a quota system was introduced in 1924 with the National Origins Formula that limited immigration to the United States from Europe, especially Eastern and Southern Europe. However, immigrants continued to flow freely from Latin America, particularly Mexico. But in 1954 a "repatriation project" organized by the US Immigration and Naturalization Service forced the deportation of thousands of Mexicans.[13] Then, in 1986, the Immigration Reform and Control Act established penalties for hiring unauthorized immigrants.

As of 2011 public opinion regarding immigration, specifically immigration from Mexico, remains split. On the one extreme is Arizona, a border state, which passed a law that "would make the failure to carry immigration documents a crime and give the police broad power to detain anyone suspected of being in the country illegally."[14] The law aims to "identify, prosecute, and deport illegal immigrants," but opponents of the law claim that it simply invites police officers to harass Hispanic-looking individuals, regardless of their citizenship status.[15] Looking Mexican essentially would be grounds enough to be stopped by a police officer. New legislation passed in Alabama goes even

further by outlawing the practice of giving illegal aliens a ride in a car. In addition, the Alabama law requires that schools establish the legal status of students' parents. Many observers consider this to be America's "most draconian anti-immigration law" and several civil rights groups are questioning its constitutionality in court.[16] On the other extreme are states, such as Minnesota, that embrace immigration. Minneapolis and St. Paul are both sanctuary cities where police officers are not allowed to stop people just to check documents. Both cities also spend considerable sums of money on assimilation programs for immigrants.[17] The hope is that diversity will increase the economic competitiveness and demographic longevity of the region.

Perhaps there would be less debate if all immigrants adapted to their new culture as effectively as did Mr. Brin. But, as Mr. Kazaryan inadvertently proves, not all do. Ironically, in the end, a country's values will decide whether to risk allowing "others" to try their luck in a new land. In any event, most Americans unquestionably will use Google to find the definition of "monoglot" and learn that "Pzo" copped a plea bargain and became simply another "thief before the law."

Notes

1. "Going to America: A Ponzi Scheme that Works," *Economist*, December 17, 2009, www.economist.com/node/15108634.
2. "Role of Immigrants in the US Labor Market," Congressional Budget Office, modified November 2005, www.cbo.gov/sites/default/files/cbofiles/ftpdocs/68xx/doc6853/11-10-immigration.pdf.
3. "Going to America."

4. Ibid.
5. Ibid.
6. Jeffrey Passel and D'Vera Cohn, "A Portrait of Unauthorized Immigrants in the United States," *Pew Research Hispanic Trends Project*, April 14, 2009, www.pewhispanic.org/2009/04/14/a-portrait-of-unauthorized-immigrants-in-the-united-states/.
7. "Going to America."

8. "The Chinese in Africa: Trying to Pull Together," *Economist*, April 20, 2011, www .economist.com/node/18586448.

9. John Prideaux, "Globalization and Immigration: Benvenuto, up to a Point," *Economist*, June 11, 2011, www.economist.com/node /18780903.

10. "Immigration: A Warmer Welcome in a Colder State," *Economist*, July 7, 2011, www.economist .com/node/18928893.

11. Theodore Roosevelt, "True American-ism," *Forum Magazine*, April 1894, http:// teachingamericanhistory.org/library/document /true-americanism-the-forum-magazine/.

12. Edward P. Hutchinson, "Immigration Policy since World War I," *Annals of the American Academy of Political and Social Science* 262 (March 1949): 15–21.

13. "Operation Wetback," Fred Koestler, *Handbook of Texas Online*, accessed May 12, 2014, www .tshaonline.org/handbook/online/articles /pgo01. Uploaded on June 15, 2010. Modified on September 4, 2013. Published by the Texas State Historical Association.

14. Randal Archibold, "Arizona Enacts Stringent Law on Immigration," *New York Times*, April 23, 2011, www.nytimes.com/2010/04/24 /us/politics/24immig.html.

15. Ibid.

16. "Illegal Immigration: Et in Alabama Ego," *Economist*, July 23, 2011, www.economist.com /node/18989121.

17. "Immigration: A Warmer Welcome in a Colder State."

Checking Comprehension

A. Based on the text, indicate whether each statement is true or false. Modify false statements to make them true.

1. According to the text, most immigrants do not integrate into the society of their new country.

2. Critics of immigration fear that America could become a "home away from home" if Americans fail to adapt to and understand the culture of immigrants.

3. One proposed method for limiting the decrease in wages for native-born workers is a protectionist policy that restricts immigration.

4. According to research carried out by the Pew Hispanic Center, Hispanic immigrants tend to work in the same sectors as native-born Americans.

5. The article implies that nearly all immigrant entrepreneurs who provide jobs to local populations benefit the local economy and population.

6. Immigration is one means to increase multilingualism in an otherwise homogeneous population.

7. Immigration is less controversial in the United States than in other countries thanks to a long tradition of "liberal" immigration policies.

8. US immigration policy changed significantly in the twentieth century due to growing anti-immigrant sentiment and such reforms as the "repatriation project."

9. Despite differences in individual states' policies and attitudes toward immigrants, citizens overwhelmingly agree with their own state's laws.

10. The author questions the value of immigrants' contribution to American society.

Mastering Vocabulary

Active Vocabulary Collocations	
Immigration and Homeland	**General**
1. border state	1. at a great cost to
2. census figures	2. liberal policy
3. cultural diversity	3. protectionist policy
4. demographic factors	4. public opinion
5. illegal aliens	5. thorny issue
6. to adapt to a new culture	6. to arouse suspicion
7. to adopt new values	7. to ban a practice
8. to check documents	8. to be/keep in touch with
9. to cross the border	9. to bring ideas to life
10. to develop loyalty	10. to enact a policy
11. to handle the influx	11. to pass a law/legislation
12. to obtain citizenship	12. to provide an opportunity
13. to preserve core cultural values	13. to question something in court
14. to resist assimilation	14. to reap what one sowed
15. to restrict/limit immigration	15. to try one's luck

Expanding Vocabulary

A. Complete the mind maps begun in the pre-reading section by using active vocabulary collocations above. In order to do this, you may need to expand your mind maps by adding new boxes and connections.

B. ⊕ Go to COCA (http://corpus.byu.edu/coca/). Click on COLLOCATES. You do not need to type anything in the box that appears. Under SORTING AND LIMITS find the dropdown menu next to MINIMUM and select MUTUAL INFO. Type each word below in the WORD(S) box and click SEARCH. Write three collocates commonly used in conjunction with each word in the left-hand column.

Foreign & Domestic Affairs	Corresponding Collocates		
1. Immigration	a. illegal	b. reform	c. policy
2. Citizenship			
3. Demographic			
4. Liberal			
5. Diversity			
6. Legislation			
7. Border			
8. Culture			
9. Assimilation			
10. Opportunity			

C. Choose five collocations concerning foreign and domestic affairs from the previous activity. Write a sentence for each collocation that either supports or condemns Arizona's immigration law, as discussed in the article.

1. _____
2. _____
3. _____
4. _____
5. _____

D. Use the Word Bank below to fill in the blanks of a passage about a legislative proposal on illegal immigrants. Not all words and word combinations will be used.

Word Bank		
illegal aliens	public opinion	law
diversity	opportunity	race
suspicion	price	borders
enactment	census	permanent residency

The DREAM (Development, Relief and Education for Alien Minors) Act is an American legislative proposal aimed at granting residency to certain (1) _____ of good moral character who graduate from US high schools, having crossed the (2) _____ of the United States as minors, and having lived in the country continuously for at least five years prior to the policy's (3) _____. An individual meeting these conditions would then apply for the DREAM Act and, once approved, do one of the following: (a) enroll in an institution of higher education in order to pursue an advanced degree or (b) enlist in one of the branches of the US military. Within six years of approval for conditional (4) _____, an individual must have completed at least two years of college studies or military service. Upon meeting all of the conditions at the end of the six-year conditional period, they would be granted permanent residency, which would eventually provide them the (5) _____ to become US citizens and contribute to the cultural (6) _____ of the country. If Congress managed to pass this (7) _____, it would target illegal immigrants up to thirty-five years of age. (8) _____ regarding this act shows that it arouses (9) _____ of a potential loophole for criminals—in particular, gang members—to legalize in the United States. As such, this act threatens to come at a great (10) _____ to society.

E. Discuss with a partner whether or not you would support the DREAM Act, as described in the previous activity. Give specific reasons for your decision.

F.   Study **Language Note 2** on definitions and examples of two commonly confused verbs, "to adapt" and "to adopt'" (from *Collins Cobuild Dictionary*).

Language Note 2	
to adapt	**to adopt**
Definition 1: If you adapt to a new situation or adapt yourself to it, you change your ideas or behavior in order to deal with it successfully. **Example:** The world will be different in the future, and we must be prepared to adapt to change. **Synonym**: to adjust	**Definition 1:** If you adopt something (a new attitude, plan, or way of behaving), you begin to have it. **Example:** Students learned to adopt a positive attitude to their new environment. **Synonym:** to take on
Definition 2: If you adapt to something, you change it to make it suitable for a new purpose or situation. **Example:** Shelves were built to adapt the office for use as a library. **Synonym:** to modify	**Definition 2:** If you adopt a country, you choose it as a place to live. **Example:** Millions adopted the United States as their new home. **Synonym:** to accept
Contrast: In some cases, in order to adapt to a new environment, a person has to adopt new values, norms, and behaviors.	

G.   Based on what you learned in Language Note 2, underline the correct variant in each sentence.

1. After the family moved to the countryside, it took them a while to (adapt/adopt) to local conditions.

2. (Adopting/Adapting) new technologies poses a challenge for conservative institutions because such technologies first have to be (adapted/adopted) to modern practices.

3. A large organization can be slow to (adapt/adopt) to change.

4. During a civil war, refugees often have to (adapt/adopt) a country, to which they struggle to (adapt/adopt).

5. (Adapting/Adopting) to driving conditions in another country can require both time and patience.

Exploring the Meaning

A. Paraphrase each sentence using appropriate active vocabulary collocations.

1. Anna was hesitant to sacrifice her Mexican heritage just to fit in better at school.
   Anna <u>resisted assimilation</u> because she valued her Mexican heritage.

2. Every year, there seem to be more and more undocumented immigrants in our country.

   _____

3. Although getting a green card can be very difficult, Jose attempted to do so and hoped for the best.

   _____

4. Whenever entering a new country, travelers must have their passports and visas checked by officials to ensure that their documents are in order.

   _____

5. Some people believe that large numbers of immigrants will only benefit the work force, but they refuse to acknowledge that there are negative aspects of immigration as well.

   _____

6. You are not allowed to enter the United States without proper documentation.

   _____

7. Arizona wants to enforce a new rule regarding illegal immigrants that has received considerable attention from the media.

   _____

8. Large numbers of immigrants have changed the socioeconomic composition of the United States.

   _____

B. Use the active vocabulary items and any other applicable collocations that might be useful when discussing immigrants and government responses to immigration.

Immigrants	Government Responses
•	•
•	•
•	•
•	•
•	•
•	•
•	•
•	•
•	•
•	•

C. With a partner, choose one of the two situations below and role-play an interview using the collocations you have written out.

Role 1: An immigrant who went on to become a famous entrepreneur gives an interview to a local TV channel about his/her life story.

Role 2: A presidential candidate responds to a local newspaper reporter's questions about his/her stance on immigration.

Discussing the Article

A. Working with a partner, use active vocabulary collocations to answer the following questions based on the text.

1. What effect does immigration have on your home country? Why is immigration an important issue regardless of where one lives?

2. What is the "American Dream?" What is its equivalent in your home country?

3. What is a "protectionist policy"? Which countries are best known for their protectionist policies?

4. Why is research related to immigration in the US so frequently focused on Hispanic immigrants? Can research about Hispanic immigrants be applied to non-Hispanic immigrants? Why or why not?

5. Which countries are typically perceived as producing the most "highly educated minds" and why? How is that perception changing?

6. Why is immigration such a controversial topic in the United States?

7. Is anti-immigration sentiment sufficient justification for anti-immigration policy? Why or why not?

8. Policies regarding immigrants in the United States vary from state to state. How might this inconsistent approach to immigration influence where immigrants choose to settle? Can this situation be found in other countries? Why or why not?

Constructing Critical Discourse

Recognizing Bias

A. "Bias" is a particular tendency or inclination that often prevents the formation of an unprejudiced opinion. The slogans below have been used at various protests around the United States. Decide whether each sign is biased toward or against immigration, what might cause that bias, and then rephrase the statement to make it unbiased, or neutral.
   1. "We are workers, not criminals"
   2. "Borders are lines drawn by racist imperialists"
   3. "Illegals have no rights, they are criminals"
   4. "The government promotes hate against Latinos"
   5. "No borders, no country"

Forming Hypotheses

A. Study the following case to determine US policy toward dual citizenship. Consider what policy your home country has in regard to dual citizenship.

Today's globalized society lends itself to qualifying for dual citizenship. Eligibility requirements include having one parent as a citizen of another country, being born in another country, or getting married to someone from another country. Some countries like China, Denmark, and Malaysia require a citizen to give up his or her citizenship if voluntarily acquiring a second. On the other hand, countries like the United States allow dual citizenship. US Chief Justice John Rutledge ruled that, although the right of citizenship under two governments is constitutional, one must symbolically renounce all prior allegiances as part of the naturalization ceremony.

B. Using the pattern shown below for constructing hypotheses, respond to the following question regarding dual citizenship.

Past conditions +	Implications for the present
• If somebody **had known** in the past, • If something **had been** true in the past, • If something **had been done** in the past,	• something **would be** different now. • something else **would happen** now. • something else **could be** different now.

1. What policy does your country have regarding dual citizenship?
   a. If dual citizenship currently is allowed, speculate on how different the social landscape of your country would be if dual citizenship had been prohibited during the previous decade.
   b. If dual citizenship currently is prohibited (or explicitly discouraged), speculate on how different the social landscape of your country would be if dual citizenship had been allowed during the previous decade.

Practice Debate

A. Choose one of the roles below and role-play it using at least ten active vocabulary items per person.
   Situation: Members of a state legislature of a border state discuss the adoption of a law aimed at tracking illegal immigrants by giving authorities the right to check suspicious individuals' documents at any time.
   Role A: A legal immigrant who has been living and working in this border state for twenty years.
   Role B: An illegal immigrant who recently left his home country to find work and support his family.

<u>Role C:</u> A representative of the border state supporting the tracking of illegal immigrants through random document checks.

<u>Role D:</u> A border patrol agent who will be authorized to inspect documents of suspicious individuals if the legislation passes.

Listening

Pre-Listening

A. Before listening to the audio file, predict the arguments that you'll hear. Fill in the table below.

Cultural preservation is more important than fostering diversity through immigration.	Fostering diversity through immigration is more important than cultural preservation.
•	•
•	•
•	•
•	•
•	•
•	•

🎧 While Listening

A. Listening for general comprehension: Listen to Audio Recording 4.2 and put a check next to arguments that appear in the table. Write down additional arguments that initially were missing in your table.

B. Listening for specific details: Listen to the audio file a second time and evaluate the arguments you listed in the table above as "strong" or "weak." Propose ways of improving the arguments you labeled as "weak."

Post-Listening

A. Which side do you think presented a more persuasive argument? Support your opinion by citing their strongest argument.

B. In every debate, someone has the last word. Predict what the opposing side's response would be to the final argument you heard.

Formatting the Argument: Writing

Writing Paragraphs

The basic rule of thumb for writing paragraphs is to limit each paragraph to one idea supported by several pieces of evidence. Sticking to one idea in a paragraph lends it unity and cohesion.

The paragraph below is both unified and cohesive. Notice how the bolded words and phrases (connectors) guide readers and show the connection between ideas.

> Advocates of stricter immigration policies have argued that immigrants are a drain on the US economy because they receive more in health care, education, and other social services than they contribute. **However**, evidence shows that immigrants, rather than draining government treasuries, add far more than they utilize in services. **First**, immigrants pay more than $90 billion in taxes annually and receive only $5 billion in welfare. **Second**, studies indicate that immigrants often contribute more than their share to the domestic economy. **For instance**, immigrants comprise one-quarter of California's population but constitute one-third of the labor force. **Moreover**, immigrants rather than nonimmigrants are 30 percent more likely to start a business in the United States, which **in turn** creates jobs for American workers. According to the Fiscal Policy Institute, small businesses owned by immigrants employed 4.7 million people and generated more than $776 billion in profits annually.

In contrast to the paragraph above, the sentences in the paragraph below, while related to one topic, represent their own ideas and are only loosely related to each other.

> Immigration reform is a priority for the federal government. America is a country of immigrants. People come to America for lots of reasons. Some immigrants end up contributing greatly to their new countries. However, the costs of illegal

immigration are enormous. Laws that allow police officers to demand documentation of citizenship from any nonwhite person have triggered several protests.

An important feature of paragraphs is the topic sentence that commonly appears at (or near) the beginning of a paragraph and introduces the main idea followed by supporting details. For example, in the above paragraph beginning with "Advocates of stricter immigration policies," the first sentence acts as the main idea.

A. The following paragraphs are missing a topic sentence. Read through each of them and draft a topic sentence.

> Paragraph 1: Many illegal immigrants who work in the United Kingdom send the money they earn to relatives in their home countries. Analysis by the Office for National Statistics found that $4.1 billion gross domestic product (GDP) was sent out of the country by migrant workers last year. This is a drain of resources that does little for economic growth in the United Kingdom. Moreover, many illegal immigrants are working off the books and, thus, are not paying taxes. A report by the British Home Office estimates that hundreds of thousands of migrants are working illegally, and estimates that up to 70 percent of them pay no taxes. Yet they use free health care, food stamps, and other services meant for seniors and low-income Britons. More than just services, illegal immigrants are also stealing wages from law-abiding British citizens. The gap between the rich and the poor in the United Kingdom is growing wider. In the last year alone, the bottom tenth of earners saw their pay increase by only 0.1 percent, while the top tenth saw their wages grow eighteen times faster. Perhaps one of the reasons that the poor are getting poorer is that illegals in this country are willing to work for so little. Why would employers pay higher wages if they can find workers who will accept minimum wage—or even less?

> Paragraph 2: The Internal Revenue service of the United States estimates that about 6 million unauthorized immigrants file income tax returns each year. Research conducted by the Congressional Budget Office suggests that roughly 50 to 75 percent of illegal immigrants pay federal, state, and local taxes. Illegal immigrants pay about $7 billion per year into Social Security. In addition, they also spend millions per year, contributing to the GDP.

B. Read the paragraph below and cross out any unnecessary sentences.

> While many opponents of liberal immigration policies argue that immigrants are a drain on the economy, a recent study by the Immigration Learning Center reveals otherwise. Immigrants come to this country for many reasons. They are less likely than citizens to access welfare and government programs. For example, about 45 percent of eligible noncitizens received food stamps last year, compared to almost 60 percent of eligible native-born citizens. Many immigrants have little education and work at low-paying jobs. Moreover, most immigrants, illegal or otherwise, pay more in taxes than they use in government services, paying nearly $80,000 more in taxes than they receive in federal, state, or local benefits over their lifetime. They are 30 percent more likely to start businesses than native-born citizens. Google, Yahoo, and eBay were all started by immigrants. Google's net worth now exceeds $200 billion. In total, immigrants contribute much more to the economy than they take away.

C. After familiarizing yourself with the transitions in **Language Note 3** below, read the following essay and (1) highlight the topic sentence of each paragraph in the body of the essay, and (2) circle connectors throughout.

Language Note 3

Connectors help readers follow your train of thought from sentence to sentence, paragraph to paragraph. Here are some common transitions:

- **To show examples:** for example, for instance, in particular, to illustrate, namely, specifically.
- **To show cause and effect:** as a result, consequently, hence, thus, therefore, accordingly, for this reason.
- **To show comparisons:** in the same way, likewise, similarly, along the same lines, in comparison, as well as.
- **To show contrasts:** on the contrary, but, however, despite, nonetheless, instead, rather, in contrast, as opposed to, at the same time, still, while.
- **To show a list of items:** in addition, equally important, among other things, furthermore, moreover, also.
- **To show a summary:** in brief, in short, in sum, on the whole, all in all.
- **To show a conclusion:** finally, ultimately, eventually, in conclusion.

Immigration: Position Paper

Despite numerous government assimilation programs designed to help transition immigrants to their new country, immigrants increasingly resist such efforts in favor of maintaining strong ties to their countries of origin. Generally speaking, immigrants resist assimilation and remain interested in creating a "home away from home," as opposed to becoming loyal, contributing citizens of their new country. This preoccupation with one's native culture negatively affects the economy of the destination country in the form of oversaturated labor markets, disproportionate allocations of government benefits, and billions of dollars leaving the country. As such, the actual and potential economic harm brought about by immigration eclipses any tangible benefits.

The claim that cultural diversity ensures economic development in a country fails to consider all sides of the story. The basic principle of supply and demand explains how wages for all will decrease if low-income immigrants flood the labor market. Simply put, more people working for less money equals fewer jobs for everyone. George Borjas of Harvard University estimates that the wages of native-born workers decrease by about 4 percent for every 10 percent increase in the number of immigrants with similar skills.[1] In light of the high unemployment rates already plaguing the US economy, there could be little if any benefit to saturating the market with cheap foreign labor.

Additionally, many immigrants, especially poor and illegal aliens, consume a large percentage of government resources in the forms of health care, welfare, and education. According to the Center for Immigration Services (CIS) regarding the 2010 US Census, a high level of illegal immigrant poverty contributes to increases in welfare programs, not to mention the fact that many who benefit from such government services fail to pay into the system by filing federal and state taxes.[2] This failure to pay income tax, for example, partly stems from employers paying undocumented immigrants below minimum wage and under the table. But when immigrants show up at the emergency room or send a child to a public school, the cost associated with caring for and educating those children remains the same. Even when they are documented, many poor immigrants turn to the welfare system to make ends meet. The CIS also pointed out that 43 percent of immigrants who lived in the United States for twenty years were receiving government assistance—a figure nearly double the rate of natural-born citizens. This disproportionate rate of consumption clearly has short- and long-term detrimental effects.

Finally, the economic practices of many immigrants negatively impact the economy of their host country. Many immigrants often work for the purpose of sending money, or remittances, back to family members in their home countries.

While some argue that this practice bears little impact on the economy of a host country, the reality is just the opposite. In fact, the Bureau of Economic Analysis estimates that around $50 billion dollars are sent out of the United States in the form of remittances each year—nearly the same amount as the government's entire foreign aid budget.[3] Such a dramatic loss of capital has particularly serious implications for a country such as the United States, whose economic system depends on internal participation. Citizens sending money home rather than contributing to the economic welfare of their host country puts the entire system in jeopardy.

In sum, lax immigration policies cannot be favored in light of the demonstrable economic harm that comes as a result. Immigrants resisting assimilation and taking advantage of the system impact the entire country. Cheap immigrant labor leads to lower-paying jobs and fewer of them, and the low-income status of many immigrants results in a veritable drain on government assistance programs. Furthermore, most of the wages earned contribute to the economies of other countries. As such, the advantages of maintaining a country's economic integrity far outweigh those associated with encouraging immigration and cultural diversity.

Notes

1. "Increasing the Supply of Labor through Immigration: Measuring the Impact on Native-born Workers," Harvard Center for Immigration Studies, modified March 2004, www.cis.org /LaborSupply-ImmigrationEffectsNatives.

2. "Task Force on New Americans Report— Building an Americanization Movement for the Twenty-first Century," Center for Immigration Services, modified September 30, 2011, www.uscis.gov/portal/site/uscis /menuitem.5af9bb95919f35e66f614176543f6d1a /?vgnextchannel=68439c7755cb9010VgnVCM 10000045f3d6a1RCRD&vgnextoid=0c63a317 cd64e110VgnVCM1000004718190aRCRD.

3. Natalie Kitroeff, "Immigrants Pay Lower Fees to Send Money Home, Helping to Ease Poverty," *New York Times*, April 28, 2013, www.nytimes.com/2013/04/28/us/politics /immigrants-find-it-cheaper-to-send-money -home.html?pagewanted=all.

Write Your Own Position Paper

A. Write a position paper on the topic "Cultural Preservation versus Diversity" that consists of five to six paragraphs. Be sure to include active vocabulary from this unit.

Formatting the Argument: Speaking

Implementing Rhetorical Strategies

A. Study the following note:

> **Strategy Note 1**   In Units 1–3, we covered the first three of the five debate strategies: conjecture, definition strategies, and cause and effect strategies.
>
>   In this unit, we will focus on the fourth strategy: **value questions**. Value questions ask whether something is good or bad, beautiful or ugly, better or worse. We examine, agree with, or challenge the qualities of an idea. You have read and talked about immigration from a "values" perspective. Those who employ this strategy typically develop a set of criteria, or points that support the value in question. For example, "Immigration is good because it leads to X, Y, and Z happening, which, everyone can agree, are good things."

B. Review the text, highlighting important value-based words or phrases that you could use to support your side of the debate. For example, if you are arguing that immigration improves a society or nation, look for words and expressions that point out positive developments that result from immigration.

    List five important value statements that support your side of the argument.

    1. _____
    2. _____
    3. _____
    4. _____
    5. _____

C. During the debate, you can use these value statements to support your argument or to weaken the argument of the other side. For instance, you could ask and answer something like, "What value do immigrants bring to a nation in terms of economic development, cultural richness, and social unity?"

    Based on the value statements or questions you have listed above, write five sentences or questions you could use in your debate.

    1. _____
    2. _____
    3. _____
    4. _____
    5. _____

D. As you prepare for the debate, you can predict that the other side will use value statements and criteria that support their side of the argument. You can argue against these statements by pointing out weaknesses in the other side's value statements. To illustrate, the other side may argue that immigration does not improve society because many immigrants believe and do things that are strange. How would you argue against such a statement?

Review the text and list five key value relationships that the other side could use to support their position. Then list how you would argue against these relationships.

1. _____
2. _____
3. _____
4. _____
5. _____

E. Review and application of previous debate strategies:

In Units 1–3, we covered the first three of the five debate strategies: conjecture, definition, and cause and effect. In preparation for the debate, apply these strategies to support your argument or weaken the argument of the other side. Plan ways to use these strategies during the debate.

Framing Templates

A. The following expressions can be used to **establish importance**. Review these framing templates and incorporate them into both your oral and written arguments.

1. X matters/is important because. . . .
2. Although X may seem trivial, it is in fact crucial in terms of today's concern about. . . .
3. Ultimately, what is at stake here is. . . .
4. Although X may seem of concern to only a small group of . . . , it should in fact concern anyone who cares about. . . .
5. It is essential to consider all sides of the story when it comes to. . . .

Dealing with Questions

A. Suppose a question was asked about X; there might be times during the debate when you need to **redirect that question**. Use the following statements in case this situation arises.
- I believe this question has more to do with X, which, unfortunately, is not my area of expertise.
- X is an issue separate and apart from what we are discussing. My focus today is on Y only.
- To provide an answer, I would have to consult Z.
- This is an interesting and complex issue that warrants input from a number of different experts.

Speaking

A. **Oral Presentation:** Prepare a three- to five-minute oral presentation arguing your position. After practicing, record your presentation and then listen to it. What areas do you need to improve on? Be prepared to give your presentation in class.

B. **Debate:** Now it's time for you to debate. Synthesize all your notes dealing with arguments, useful active vocabulary collocations, and framing templates to assist you during the actual debate. Remember that these will serve as a reference only, not as a text to be read directly during your debate.

Reflection

Self-Evaluation

A. Think back over the work you have done thus far. Plot your responses to the following statements on the scale.
1. I felt prepared to debate this topic.
2. I was motivated to debate this topic.
3. I put a lot of effort into preparing to debate this topic.

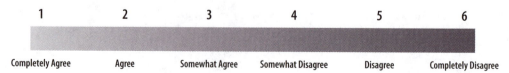

1	2	3	4	5	6
Completely Agree	Agree	Somewhat Agree	Somewhat Disagree	Disagree	Completely Disagree

B. If most of your answers were at the right end of the spectrum, what can you do to move to the left end? If most of your answers were at the left end of the spectrum, what can you do to stay in that area?

Vocabulary Recall

Identify **ten** active vocabulary collocations you have learned and used in this chapter that you feel were most beneficial to you as you debated.

1. _____
2. _____
3. _____
4. _____
5. _____
6. _____
7. _____
8. _____
9. _____
10. _____

UNIT
5

Security versus Freedom

Hawks and Doves at War

Pre-Reading

Introducing the Issue

A. With a partner, discuss your responses to the following questions regarding transportation security.

1. Describe the process of going through security at an airport or train station. If you haven't experienced this personally, use the image to make speculations.

2. What changes do you think should be made to transportation security? What would be the positive and negative effects of these changes?

3. To what extent are security officers justified in invading personal privacy to ensure general safety? Defend your answer.

B. Study **Language Note 1** on the meaning of "security" and "freedom" from the *Oxford American Dictionary and Thesaurus* and explain how you think these concepts are complementary or contradictory.

Language Note 1	
Security	**Freedom**
• the state of being free from danger or threat *Knowing that the house was locked and the alarm system activated gave the parents a sense of security.* • the safety of a state or organization against criminal activity such as terrorism, theft, or espionage *Terrorism poses a grave threat to national security and the lives of individuals around the world.* • procedures followed or measures taken to ensure such safety *Amid tight security, the presidents of several nations met to discuss drug violence in the border region.* • the state of feeling safe, stable, and free from fear or anxiety *Her lifelong friend gave her the emotional security she desperately needed.*	• the power or right to act, speak, or think as one wants without hindrance or restraint *The instructor encouraged freedom of thought and expression in the classroom.* • the absence of subjection to foreign domination or despotic government *The brave soldiers put their lives in harm's way and championed the cause of freedom.* • the state of not being imprisoned or enslaved *The shark thrashed its way to freedom.* • the freedom from the state of not being subject to or affected by a particular undesirable thing *Government welfare policies promote freedom from want.* • the unrestricted use of something *Owing to the wet spring, homeowners had the freedom to water their lawns as they pleased.*

C. Study the information below and analyze the title "Hawks and Doves at War."

Hawks: People who believe in using force and aggressive or warlike policies to resolve conflicts.

Doves: People who advocate peaceful and diplomatic methods of conflict resolution.

D. Make a list of issues that might be discussed in this article based on your analysis of the title.

1. _____

2. _____

3. _____

4. _____

5. _____

Creating Mind Maps

A. Brainstorm as many words as you know associated with the challenges a country might face regarding security and freedom. Arrange your ideas to create two separate mind maps according to the pattern shown below. After reading the article, you will be able to add more information, so leaving boxes blank at this point is okay.

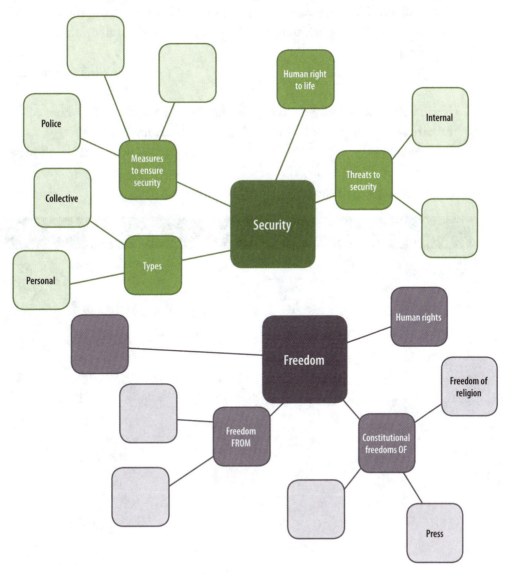

B. Compare your maps with those of your classmates to generate additional ideas. After completing each of the two maps, decide which topic areas can help bridge the gap between the two maps. In other words, which issues concerning security and freedom intersect?

Discussing Facts and Opinions

A. Read the two quotations below. What kinds of freedom and security are discussed in each quote?

> True individual freedom cannot exist without economic security and independence. People who are hungry and out of a job are the stuff of which dictatorships are made.
>
> Franklin D. Roosevelt

> If you want total security, go to prison. There you're fed, clothed, given medical care and so on. The only thing lacking . . . is freedom.
>
> Dwight D. Eisenhower

B. Make a list of all possible kinds of security and freedom.

Freedom	Security
•	•
•	•
•	•
•	•
•	•
•	•

C. Taking into consideration all possible kinds of freedom and security, explain the meaning of the following quotation. Do you agree or disagree with it? Provide your reasons.

> Those who surrender freedom for security will not have, nor do they deserve, either one.
>
> Thomas Jefferson

Studying the Topic

Focused Reading

A. As you read "Hawks and Doves at War," list the arguments for both sides of the debate in the following table.

Limiting Freedoms for the Sake of Security	Upholding Freedoms at the Expense of Security
•	•
•	•
•	•
•	•
•	•
•	•
•	•
•	•
•	•
•	•

B. 🎧 Check your pronunciation of unfamiliar words from the text as you listen to Audio Recording 5.1.

Hawks and Doves at War

Grant Newman

Terrorists employ highly unconventional methods in their efforts to breach security and take advantage of others' freedom. Richard Reid, a Brit, hid a bomb in his shoe before boarding an airplane in Paris bound for Miami in December 2001. Umar Farouk Abdulmutallab, a Nigerian, used his underwear to conceal a bomb while en route to Detroit eight years later in December 2009. While both attempts failed due to technical malfunctions, they nevertheless incited a vigorous debate between "hawks," who called for a tightening of personal freedoms in order to ensure security, and "doves," who retorted that personal freedoms are already tight enough and that, if anything, a loosening of personal freedoms is needed. Such a disagreement reinforces the ongoing debate as to whether governments, in their efforts to ensure security from terrorism, have gone too far in invading personal freedoms or have failed to go far enough.

Privacy campaigners are concerned about the invasion on liberty proposed by risk-based security screening in airports. In theory, the process involves using an individual's history to assess the potential security risk he or she poses to the transportation system and to design a specially adapted screening process for him or her. Because privacy laws restrict government access to personal information, security departments contract private companies to gather information on individuals and to offer recommendations to agents; the government makes a decision based on an individual's information ostensibly without ever handling the information itself. The underlying effect is that so-deemed low-risk individuals receive different treatment than high-risk individuals. Bennet Waters, president of CLEAR, a company that gathers personal information for such purposes, remarked, "If you look at some combination of government data and commercially available data . . . you can begin to build a more fulsome picture of a traveler's relative risk to aviation security."[1] Notes from a Transport Canada briefing reveal a discussion about how risk-based security screening does entail "complex operational, policy, legal, privacy, and human rights dimensions."[2] Although such a system would enable the government to identify so-called clear skins—individuals on whom the government has no information whatsoever—civil rights activists suggest that government is wrongly sidestepping privacy laws and therefore going too far in invading personal liberties.

Critics of government actions to ensure security from terrorism suggest that officials in legal systems are abusing the rights and liberties of the accused. Civil rights activists have plenty of objections in the West, where Britain's dovish Liberal Democrats are furious with their more hawkish coalition partners, the Tories, who would restrict the rights of foreign terror suspects in Britain. Due to technicalities and supposed security threats, the government finds its hands tied regarding these suspects; neither can the government prosecute suspects immediately, nor can it allow them to leave the country for security purposes and, therefore, issues control orders. Without even hearing the evidence against them, supposed terrorists are subject to restrictions on telephone and internet usage, close surveillance, electronic tagging, strict curfews, and limitations on travel, if not total relocation. Although positive changes to the system now allow a suspect to at least understand the gist of the evidence against him or her, a component of personal freedom is still lacking.[3] Civil rights activists echo Edmund Burke, an eighteenth-century British statesman, who once suggested, "Liberty, if I understand it at all, is a general principle, and the clear right of all the subjects within the realm. Partial freedom seems to me a most invidious mode of slavery."[4]

Countering the arguments against further encroachment on liberties, proponents of heightened security measures cite government's failure to thwart terrorist attacks as reason enough to further restrict personal freedoms. They argue that in a digital age, government needs to do even more to ensure the security of its citizens. Ivan Zassoursky, chief editor at Chaskor.ru, a Russian-language news website, points to internet monitoring as a prophylactic measure for fighting terrorism. "Many problems could have been avoided if the Internet had already been monitored for several years and if all individuals expressing [truly] extreme views . . . were identified and on the books of competent authorities," Zassoursky remarks.[5] Even

a cursory look at the internet postings of Anders Breivik, the bomber and gunman in the Norwegian terrorist attack of July 22, 2011, suggests that trouble lurked. A more attentive government might have noticed this and prevented the tragic deaths of sixty-nine individuals.

Security hawks also fear that some countries essentially encourage terrorist attacks by failing to punish perpetrators sufficiently. The aforementioned tragedy in Norway further suggests that government is perhaps falling short. If convicted, Mr. Breivik might spend his prison sentence in what Fox News, an American news television station, calls a "heavenly prison," offering individual rooms for each inmate complete with ceramic tile and flatscreen TVs. True, by sending Mr. Breivik to such a facility, the Norwegian government has removed a wrongdoer from society. However, American observers are concerned as to "whether a comfortable . . . detention is sufficient to deter similar crimes."[6] A guilty verdict and a comparatively plush incarceration for Breivik might set a precedent for future terrorists, who might simply need to establish Norway as their jurisdiction in order to ensure a velvety sentence for any act committed, no matter how deadly. As one American commented on Facebook, "If you prefer comfort to liberty, go to Norway and commit murder. You could get 21 years in what looks like a nice dorm."[7] Many observers feel that such a punishment lacks justice and that a government providing such an option to potential terrorists is not going far enough to ensure security.

Ideally, establishing justice, ensuring domestic tranquility, and securing liberty is precisely the purpose of the US Constitution as set forth in its Preamble. Many Americans even become misty-eyed when discussing the liberties canonized in their Constitution. Patrick Henry, a founder of the United States, famously cried, "Give me liberty or give me death," while Benjamin Franklin, another founder, much more calmly wrote, "They that can give up essential liberty to obtain a little temporary safety deserve neither liberty nor safety." Thanks to a long-standing constitution and ensuing legal precedent, discussion of liberties in the United States is rarely hypothetical and often highly practical, being based on actual events and court decisions.

During the American Civil War, Abraham Lincoln suspended habeas corpus, a legal writ protected in the US Constitution requiring that a judge approve all arrests after considering evidence against an arrestee. ✪ Since the 9/11 terrorist attacks, habeas corpus has been suspended again for "high-risk" members of society. Notwithstanding, in 2008, the US Supreme Court monumentally ruled in *Boumediene v. Bush* that the right to challenge the constitutional legality of one's detention by invoking habeas corpus extends even to inmates housed at the Guantanamo Bay Naval Base detention camp.[8] Thus, although the government infringes upon this right, the courts act as a check on such infringement.

Furthermore, the Fourth Amendment to the US Constitution guarantees the right of the people against unreasonable search and seizure. Peter Moskos, a former Baltimore police officer and a professor at John Jay College in New York, cites abuse in the United States of the implied-consent principle and the principle of plain-view searches—two closely tied principles regarding search and seizure.[9] First, zones of implied consent, including airports and train stations, where citizens tacitly consent to being searched without a warrant, are widening to such areas as public streets and subways. Second, plain-view searches, which involve police officers collecting physical evidence from a suspect without a warrant if the item is in plain view, are being used to inspect for non-terror-related contraband, including so-called suspicious items that are not necessarily dangerous, such as "large amounts of cash, pirated CDs, pornography and, of course, drugs."[10] Moskos reasons, "Of course people shouldn't break the law or carry illegal objects. But the difference between civilian employees searching for bombs in airports and government agents conducting random searches for suspicious objects is the difference between preserving a free society and creating a police state."[11] The US Supreme Court has facilitated the expanding powers of police officers by allowing searches based merely on "reasonable grounds" rather than the constitutionally mandated "probable cause."[12]

Ultimately, a respectable government will endeavor to strike a balance between liberties and security. Commenting on the thoughts of Sir David Omand, a British former intelligence and security coordinator for Tony Blair, the *Economist* opines,

"Governments must be able to show that they are doing everything that is reasonable to protect citizens from threats, but they must be candid in admitting that not all risks can be eliminated without doing more harm than good and eroding the very values they are seeking to defend."[13] Until such a balance is struck between security and liberty, the likes of Patrick Henry might receive both sides of his ultimatum, while the likes of Benjamin Franklin might lose both.

Notes

1. "Aviation Security: CLEAR Ahead," *Economist*, August 8, 2011, www.economist.com/blogs/gulliver/2011/08/aviation-security.

2. "Privacy Czar Slams Airport Screening Plan," *Canadian Press*, August 30, 2011, www.cbc.ca/news/politics/privacy-czar-slams-airport-screening-plan-1.1096457.

3. "Dealing with Suspected Terrorists: Last Orders?," *Economist*, January 6, 2011, www.economist.com/node/17857381.

4. "Liberty v Security: The Decline of the Great Writ," *Economist*, April 15, 2010, www.economist.com/node/15905883.

5. Ivan Zassoursky, "Nenavist na Uchiote," *New Times*, August 8, 2011, translated by Grant Newman, http://newtimes.ru/articles/detail/42004/.

6. "Norwegian v American Justice: Plush and Unusual Punishment," *Economist*, July 28, 2011, www.economist.com/blogs/democracyinamerica/2011/07/norwegian-v-american-justice.

7. Ibid.

8. "Liberty v Security: The Decline of the Great Writ," *Economist*, April 15, 2010, www.economist.com/node/15905883.

9. Peter Moskos, "Balancing Security and Liberty," *Washington Post*, August 2, 2004, www.washingtonpost.com/wp-dyn/articles/A33132-2004Aug1.html.

10. Ibid.

11. Ibid.

12. "Lexington: Save the Fourth Amendment," *Economist*, May 12, 2011, www.economist.com/node/18681714.

13. "Intelligence Gathering: A Question of Balance," *Economist*, July 8, 2010, www.economist.com/node/16537018.

Checking Comprehension

A. Select the most appropriate answer for each question.

1. The main purpose of this article is to
   a. argue against comfortable living conditions in prison.
   b. discuss security issues that have arisen since 9/11.
   c. explore the difficult task of balancing safety and freedom.
   d. differentiate between doves and hawks.

2. Which of the following is mentioned in the article as an argument for infringing on personal freedom to increase security?
   a. Police searches are based only on "reasonable grounds."
   b. Pursuing safety causes more harm than good.
   c. The government is unable to stop terrorist attacks.
   d. Officials are abusing the liberties of the accused.

3. Concerning the Norwegian bomber's incarceration, one American wrote, "If you prefer comfort to liberty, go to Norway and commit murder." Based on this statement, you can infer that this particular American wants
   a. all terrorists to relocate to Norway.
   b. a comfortable life regardless of liberty.
   c. to be uncomfortable so as to be free.
   d. harsher punishments against terrorists.

4. Patrick Henry cried, "Give me liberty or give me death." Based on this quote we can assume that he was a
   a. Republican.
   b. dove.
   c. hawk.
   d. Democrat.

5. Which sentence fits best at the ✪ in the seventh paragraph?
   a. Lincoln was the sixteenth president of the United States, and his life was tragically cut short when he was assassinated at the age of fifty-six.
   b. Lincoln did so in order to protect the capital, Washington, DC, which he felt was in danger of being surrounded by hostile forces.
   c. Even in the early years of the United States, leaders understood that personal freedoms were more important than absolute security.
   d. Ensuring the safety of citizens and simultaneously respecting their personal freedoms remains a difficult task to accomplish today.

6. The difference between airport security searching for weapons and police officers searching homes and cars for suspicious items is the difference between
   a. protecting public safety and totalitarianism.
   b. preserving freedom and anarchy.
   c. invasion of personal privacy and security.
   d. maintaining liberty and nonchalance.

Mastering Vocabulary

Active Vocabulary Collocations	
Liberty and Security	**General**
1. access to personal information	1. a grim picture
2. civil rights activists	2. to express views
3. heightened security measures	3. to assess the potential risk
4. to abuse rights	4. to be closely tied to something
5. to conduct random searches	5. to eliminate risks
6. to deter crimes	6. to fall short
7. to ensure security/safety	7. to find/have one's hands tied
8. to establish justice	8. to go to great lengths
9. to gather information/data on individuals	9. to go too far in doing something
10. to infringe on/upon the right	10. to incite a vigorous debate
11. to invade personal freedoms	11. to provide an option
12. to thwart terrorist attacks	12. to reinforce the ongoing debate
13. to restrict the rights	13. to set a precedent
14. police state	14. to strike a balance between
15. unreasonable search and seizure	15. (un)conventional methods

Expanding Vocabulary

A. Complete the mind maps begun in the pre-reading section by using active vocabulary collocations above. In order to do this, you may need to expand your mind maps by adding new boxes and connections.

B. ⊕ Select the collocate that does <u>NOT</u> correspond to each vocabulary word. To do this, go to COCA (http://corpus.byu.edu/coca/) and click on COLLOCATES, then type "[v*]" in the box that appears. Under SORTING AND LIMITS find the drop-down menu next to MINIMUM and select MUTUAL INFO. Type each word in the WORD(S) box and click SEARCH.

Liberty & Security	Corresponding Collocates			
1. Rights	a. protect	b. leave	c. violate	d. reserve
2. Safety	a. assure	b. usher	c. guarantee	d. enhance
3. Search	a. clean	b. conduct	c. stop	d. perform
4. Freedoms	a. enjoy	b. defend	c. pretend	d. grant
5. Risks	a. outweigh	b. take	c. reduce	d. handle
6. Debate	a. spin	b. center	c. continue	d. spark
7. Justice	a. investigate	b. deny	c. engage	d. obstruct
8. Crime	a. reduce	b. fight	c. commit	d. do
9. Precedent	a. establish	b. set	c. enter	d. follow
10. Security	a. provide	b. emulate	c. guarantee	d. tighten

C. Fill in the blanks with the appropriate corresponding collocate for each bolded vocabulary word, as found in the previous activity.

1. The new airport body scanners will surely _____ a heated **debate** regarding personal privacy.
2. Schools may decide to make some changes and _____ **security** in light of the recent school shooting.
3. Governments that tap citizens' phone lines are not ashamed to _____ people's **rights**.
4. The customs officers decided to _____ a **search** of the suitcases and identified undeclared goods.

5. We need to protest government-sponsored telephone tapping so as to _____ our **freedoms**.

6. We're trying to _____ a **precedent** that you don't have to violate personal privacy to provide safety.

D. Write five sentences either supporting or condemning privacy laws restricting government access to personal information, such as finances, phone logs, and email accounts. Each sentence must contain at least one active vocabulary collocation and one corresponding collocation from activity B in this section.

1. _____

2. _____

3. _____

4. _____

5. _____

E. Match the synonyms in columns A and B.

Column A	Column B
1. to deter	a. to limit
2. to ensure	b. to stop
3. to infringe	c. to articulate
4. to thwart	d. to prevent
5. to restrict	e. to link
6. to express	f. to offer
7. to tie	g. to guarantee
8. to provide	h. to collect
9. to gather	i. to breach
10. to assess	j. to evaluate

F. Study **Language Note 2** regarding definitions and examples of two commonly confused verbs: "to access" and "to assess" (from the *Oxford English Dictionary*). Underline the correct variant in each of the following sentences.

Language Note 2	
To access	**To assess**
1. To approach or enter (a place) *He wasn't able to gain access to the school because it was locked.* 2. To obtain, examine, or retrieve (data or a file) *I need to access the files in your computer.*	1. To evaluate or estimate the nature, ability, or quality *I need to assess his qualifications before I can hire him.* 2. To estimate the price or value *After the car crash, I was too nervous to assess the damage.*

1. Many social websites have open (access/assess) and therefore cannot guarantee users' privacy.
2. You can often (access/assess) the quality of airport safety based on the number of security breaches.
3. Many institutions reserve the right to restrict (access/assess) to potentially threatening websites.
4. The US Senate Committee on Homeland Security released a report that attempted to (access/assess) the cost of safety.
5. We can (access/assess) his character by offering him (access/assess) to classified information and then observing his actions.

Exploring the Meaning

A. Fill in the table below by grouping active vocabulary collocations according to their connotation.

Positive	Context-Dependent	Negative
•	•	•
•	•	•
•	•	•
•	•	•
•	•	•
•	•	•

B. Recently, there was an explosion at the train station in City X. Rumor has it that this was an intentional attack and that the mayor recently called a press conference. Using active vocabulary collocations from the above table, formulate five questions you could ask the mayor regarding the situation.

1. _____
2. _____
3. _____
4. _____
5. _____

Discussing the Article

A. Working with a partner, use active vocabulary collocations to answer the following questions based on the text.

1. According to the article, what is meant by "a specially adapted screening process?" Is it fair to have different screening processes for higher-risk individuals? Why or why not?

2. What freedoms should a government restrict for suspected criminals? Should the nature of a crime determine the freedoms a government restricts? Why or why not?

3. What evidence, if any, should the government provide in order to justly detain those accused of terrorist crimes?

4. The author points out that "even a cursory look at the internet postings of Anders Breivik . . . [would have] suggested that trouble lurked." Had the Norwegian government seen his posts, would this information have been enough to prevent Breivik's attack? Why or why not?

5. What is habeas corpus? Should it exist in all countries? Why or why not? When, if ever, is the suspension of rights like habeas corpus justified?

6. The judicial branch in the United States retains a check on the executive branch. In your opinion, is such a system of checks and balances relevant to questions of liberty and security in other nations?

7. Can rights change over time? Why or why not?

8. Should individual citizens be allowed to carry items such as large amounts of cash and pornography without being searched? Why or why not? Who ought to decide what constitutes "probable cause" in such situations?

9. The final paragraph concludes that governments must do what they can to protect their citizens without going so far that they infringe on individual liberties. Is this possible? Why or why not?

10. If you had to forfeit one for the other, would you rather limit your country's security or your individual liberty? How might answers to this question vary according to country?

Constructing Critical Discourse

Recognizing Logical Fallacies

A. In debates, people use various types of logic to argue their point. Some argumentative strategies are weaker than others and should generally be avoided. Study the table below and familiarize yourself with weak argumentative strategies, known as logical fallacies.

Explanation	Example
Bandwagon Appeal	
Because everyone believes and/or does something it must be true/right	*You shouldn't assign so much homework because none of my other teachers do.*
Circular Logic	
Supporting a premise with a premise rather than a conclusion	*Johnson is the most successful mayor of the town because he's the best mayor in our history!*
Faulty Analogy	
Assuming that because two things are alike in one or more respects, they are alike in some other respect	*Making people register their guns is like the Nazis making the Jews register with the government.*
Hasty Generalization	
Making broad statements that something is true/right based on insufficient or limited evidence	*I saw two white squirrels in New York. All squirrels in New York are white.*
Red Herring	
Introducing irrelevant or distracting issues to support an argument	*I don't deserve a C on this paper. I'm the captain on the soccer team.*

B. Now read the following statements and decide if they are logically sound or faulty. If you discover a logical fallacy, identify what type it is.

1. There should be harsher punishments for terrorists because we need to dissuade others from pursuing the same actions.
2. Both times I've gone to the airport, security has searched the contents of my bags. I am the only one security ever checks.
3. There is only one metal detector that everyone at my school has to pass through each morning. We could all get in quicker if they purchased another metal detector.
4. I shouldn't have to go through security checks. I'm a white, middle-class American.
5. When police officers ask for your license and registration, it's like asking to see your underwear. Both are private things cops have no right to see.
6. Government agents should have the right to monitor our finances for suspicious activity because they're the government.
7. I'm willing to be more open about my personal information because I want to live in a safe country.
8. China shouldn't monitor its citizens' internet searches since other countries don't.

Forming Hypotheses

A. Study the following case to determine search methods used by airport security officials.

In an attempt to ensure passenger security, airport officials employ a variety of search methods, including metal detectors, x-ray machines, baggage search, prohibition of liquids and sharp items in carry-ons, mandatory shoe removal, biometrics checks, luggage screening, passenger profiling, interrogation of travelers, random checks, and the like.

B. Using the pattern shown below for constructing hypotheses, respond to the following scenarios regarding travel security.

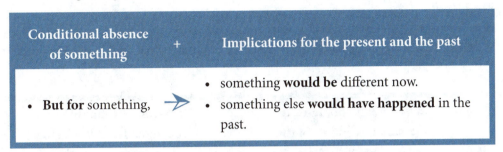

Conditional absence of something	+	Implications for the present and the past
• **But for** something,	→	• something **would be** different now. • something else **would have happened** in the past.

1. Imagine a situation in which one or more of the previously mentioned search methods are forgone. Consider both a favorable scenario, for example, respecting privacy or saving time, and an unfavorable scenario, for example, increasing the possibility of threats or encouraging disturbance.

Practice Debate

A. Choose one of the roles below and role-play it using at least ten active vocabulary collocations per person.

Situation: An anonymous email came to the head of security at a large business center saying that one of the employees might pose a threat to the security of the building. The name was not provided. An emergency meeting was called to determine the best course of action to pursue.

Role A: You are the head of security responsible for working out a plan to deal with the situation. Ask the participants for suggestions and, following the discussion, make the final decision.

Role B: You are an expert in conflict resolution in corporate settings. Propose measures to prevent potential danger to those in the building.

Role C: You are a specialist in the information technology department at the center. Bring your expertise to the discussion on what to do.

Role D: You are a representative of a major corporation headquartered in the building. You are concerned about your employees' reaction to a possible infringement on their civil rights.

Listening

Pre-Listening

A. Before listening to the audio file, predict the arguments that you'll hear. Fill in the table below.

Governments should restrict personal freedoms in the interest of security.	Governments should uphold personal freedoms at the expense of security.
•	•
•	•
•	•
•	•
•	•
•	•
•	•

While Listening

A. **Listening for general comprehension:** Listen to Audio Recording 5.2 and put a check next to arguments that appear in the table. Write down additional arguments that initially were missing in your table.

B. **Listening for specific details:** Listen to the audio file a second time and evaluate the arguments you listed in the table above as "strong" or "weak." Propose ways of improving the arguments you labeled as "weak."

Post-Listening

A. Which side do you think presented a more persuasive argument? Support your opinion by citing their strongest argument.

B. In every debate, someone has the last word. Predict what the opposing side's response would be to the final argument you heard.

Formatting the Argument: Writing

Formulating Introductions and Conclusions

Introduction: The aim of the introduction is to state clearly your position on an issue; however, capturing the reader's attention comes first. As such, your introduction will conclude with the thesis statement, and the rest of the paragraph should logically lead to that claim.

An introduction can open with the following attention grabbers:

1. *An intriguing example.* Several of the essays in this textbook begin with interesting anecdotes: In Unit 1, Brooke Ward begins with logging in Brazil to illustrate the conflict between environmental protection and economic growth. In the essay "Hawks and Doves at War," Grant Newman introduces the topic of security and civil liberties with several examples of terrorists who have attempted to sneak explosives aboard planes in unusual ways.
2. *A startling statistic that illustrates the seriousness of the problem you are addressing.* For example, in an essay on redistribution of wealth, you might begin by noting that X percent of the population owns X percent of the wealth.
3. *A provocative quotation.* For example, Benjamin Franklin stated that "They that can give up essential liberty to obtain a little temporary safety deserve neither liberty nor safety."
4. *A thought-provoking question.* Is it ever justifiable to curtail civil liberties? or What is the price of security?

A. Read the introductory paragraphs of each essay in this textbook. Identify the strategies used to draw the reader's attention. Which do you find most effective?

B. Read each of the introductory paragraphs below and critique them. Which of them provide an effective hook? Which do not? Why not?

1. The question of civil liberties and security is very important. There are many different aspects to the problem. Some people feel that security is more important than civil liberties, while others feel that civil liberties are the most important.

2. Two years ago passengers in a German airport stripped to their underwear to protest the introduction of intrusive body scanners. Calling themselves a "fleshmob," the protestors wore slogans on their bodies, such as "Something to hide?" or "Be a good citizen—drop your pants." The new scanners, dubbed "virtual strip searches" by critics, allow security personnel to see beneath a person's clothing. The German protestors were angry that their persons were being violated so that the state could reduce the risk of terrorism. In doing so, they rightfully exercised their civil liberties and demonstrated the need to curtail government intrusion into personal privacy.

3. Life, liberty, and the pursuit of happiness are all God-given rights, as stated in the "Declaration of Independence." Liberty is defined in the *American Heritage Dictionary* as "the condition of being free from restriction or control, and the right and power to act, believe, or express oneself in a manner of one's own choosing." Americans have never been liberated truly. The government has always had some sort of laws and regulations to restrict and control us from total liberty.

4. How can governments effectively protect their citizens from terrorism without infringing on their civil liberties? Many in the United States would argue that no infringement on personal privacy and civil liberties is ever justified. Yet what use are civil liberties to citizens who died as the result of a preventable terrorist act? To live in a secure nation, Americans must be willing to sacrifice basic freedoms guaranteed in the Bill of Rights.

5. On February 27, 1933, an arsonist burned down the Reichstag building in Germany. The very next day, the Reichstag Fire Decree, proposed by Adolf Hitler, was adopted. This decree suspended most civil liberties in Germany. Many believe that it was this decree that paved the way for Hitler's assumption to power. The provisions of the Reichstag Fire Decree are strikingly similar to those of the PATRIOT Act, enacted within weeks of the terrorist attacks on the World Trade Center. And the purported purpose of both laws was to protect citizens from further violence. The broad powers afforded the federal government by the PATRIOT Act should be abolished to ensure the survival of our democratic freedoms.

Conclusion: The purpose of a conclusion also is twofold: (1) to summarize the key points and restate the thesis and (2) to reinforce the claim with a final thought. The conclusion should not contain any new information or unsupported claims.

The following strategies help to frame the final thought:

1. Asking a final rhetorical question
2. Using a quotation or referring back to the original question
3. Making a prediction
4. Suggesting consequences
5. Making a recommendation

C. Read the following examples of introductory and concluding paragraphs and
   (a) observe the way in which thesis statements are restated and (b) determine the type
   of strategy used for attention grabbers and final thoughts.

Introductory Paragraph	Concluding Paragraph
On February 27, 1933, an arsonist burned down the Reichstag building in Germany. The very next day, the Reichstag Fire Decree, proposed by Adolf Hitler, was adopted. This decree suspended most civil liberties in Germany. Many believe that it was this decree that paved the way for Hitler's assumption of power. The provisions of the Reichstag Fire Decree are strikingly similar to those of the PATRIOT Act, enacted within weeks of the terrorist attacks on the World Trade Center. And the alleged purpose of both laws was to protect citizens from further violence. The broad powers afforded the federal government by the PATRIOT Act should be abolished to ensure the survival of our democratic freedoms.	The PATRIOT Act allows the government to stomp on the basic rights guaranteed by the Constitution. Winston Churchill noted, "The power of the Executive to cast a man into prison without formulating any charge known to the law and particularly to deny him the judgment of his peers is in the highest degree odious and is the foundation of all totalitarian government." As such, it should be abolished.

D. Read the following essay. Highlight the thesis statement. What strategy does the
   author use to attract the reader's attention to it? How is the thesis statement restated in
   the conclusion? Which method of presenting the final thought is used?

Security versus Freedom: Position Paper

A government's main responsibility is to protect its people. James A. Garfield, the twentieth president of the United States, said it best when he stated, "the chief duty of government is to keep the peace." This quote embodies a long-standing principle of American governance. When deciding the future of the American colonies, the Founding Fathers looked to political philosopher John Locke's writings on the social contract for guidance. According to his theory, people agreed to give up certain rights and freedoms in exchange for the protection of their lives, liberty, and property. Put another way, the entire reason why governments exist is to ensure the safety of their citizens. It was upon this idea that the entire system of American government was built and has survived for nearly three hundred years. Compromising on this most basic principle would not only undermine the theory behind our political system but could lead to more acts of terrorism and deaths.

Some people suggest that allowing a government to limit any personal freedoms will ultimately cause our country to become a police state where the government is aware of every aspect of our lives. On the other hand, the dangers our country faces today are graver than they have ever been. In December of 2012 Scott McClellan, a White House spokesperson, stated that the Department of Homeland Security observed a recent surge in the volume of terrorist threats when compared to previous years, and he encouraged everyone to be on a "heightened state of alert."[1] The requirement that society surrender some personal freedoms is a small price to pay to ensure the safety of all. Since the infamous attacks of September 11, 2001, terrorists have come in all shapes and sizes, carrying weapons in everything from their shoes to their underwear. When an enemy combatant dresses, talks, and acts like an ordinary citizen, the threat of their presence is constant. Because the threat is constant, the best way to address the situation is through heightened security measures. This minimal infringement on a person's privacy is the sacrifice required in exchange for their protection.

Furthermore, as terrorists continue to update their tactics, the government should do the same. Governments around the world have continuously fallen short when it comes to thwarting terrorist attacks due largely to lax and inflexible security. From 2002 to 2012, more than 1,500 individual terrorist attacks were reported across the globe.[2] Most of these attacks involved shootings and bombings that took place after the terrorist had crossed a security checkpoint.[3] The terrorists' use of advanced weapons and technology makes them more dangerous and requires that our security measures adapt and heighten accordingly. As Ivan Zassoursky, chief editor at Chaskor.ru, a Russian-language news website, has pointed out, "Many problems could have been avoided if the Internet had already been monitored for several years and if all individuals expressing [truly] extreme views . . . were identified and on the books of competent authorities." Even a cursory look at the internet postings of Anders Breivik, the bomber and gunman in the Norwegian terrorist attack of July 22, 2011, suggests subversive activity. A more attentive government might have noticed this and prevented the tragic deaths of sixty-nine individuals. While proponents of personal freedoms argue that terrorists do not pose any real threat to society, there is no reason to believe their claim that security could be lessened while maintaining the same level of safety.

Opponents to appropriate increases in security measures will likely call upon the Fourth Amendment of the US Constitution for support, which guarantees against unreasonable searches and seizures. While it may seem reasonable to turn to the Constitution when addressing the topic of personal freedoms, it is important to consider the following: The Fourth Amendment guarantees against *unreasonable* searches and seizures, meaning that so long as a search is reasonable, it is constitutional. Most people in the United States would likely agree that protecting against future terrorist attacks provides a reasonable basis for searching a person.

The US Declaration of Independence paraphrases the words of John Locke in saying that all men have the right to life, liberty, and the pursuit of happiness. In order to ensure that all citizens are guaranteed these rights, a government must occasionally restrict the rights of some to eliminate the risk of harm to others and their ability to exercise their rights.

Notes

1. "Terror Threats to US Cities Reported," Richard Esposito, ABC News, modified December 19, 2012, http://abcnews.go.com/US/story?id=90132&page=1.
2. "Terrorism Incidents and Significant Dates Calendar," Lawson Terrorism Information Center, January 2013, http://archive.is/Um10F.
3. Lauren O'Brien, "The Evolution of Terrorism since 9/11," *Federal Bureau of Investigation*, September 2011, www.fbi.gov/stats-services /publications/law-enforcement-bulletin /september-2011/the-evolution-of-terrorism -since-9-11.

E. Write introductory and concluding paragraphs to your own essay and share them with your classmates. Make revisions based on their comments.

Write Your Own Position Paper

A. Write a position paper on the topic "Security versus Freedom" that consists of five to six paragraphs. Be sure to include active vocabulary collocations from this unit.

Formatting the Argument: Speaking

Implementing Rhetorical Strategies

A. Study the following note:

> **Strategy Note 1**   In Units 1–4, we covered the first four of the five debate strategies: conjecture, definition strategies, cause and effect strategies, and strategies based on values.
>
> In this unit, we will focus on the fifth strategy: **procedural questions**. Procedural questions focus on the future by extending an argument into a future reality and questioning how feasible, plausible, or credible that future may be. You have read and talked about the balance between security and freedom. Most discussions that use a procedural argument will talk about what kind of world we will have if we have too much security, too little freedom, or the alternatives. For example, one side could describe what living in a nation would be like if security were seen as more important than personal freedoms.

B. Review the text highlighting important words or phrases that you could use to support your side of the debate. For example, if you are arguing that implementing a freedom-first philosophy is best, you could look for words and phrases that may be used to describe a way of life where freedom is more important than security.

List five important procedural statements that support your side of the argument.

1. _____
2. _____
3. _____
4. _____
5. _____

C. During the debate, you can use these procedural statements to support your argument or to weaken the argument of the other side. For instance, you could ask and answer something like, "How would we live in a nation where security is seen as far more important than freedom?"

Based on the procedural statements you have listed above, write five sentences or questions you could use in your debate.

1. _____
2. _____
3. _____

4. _____

5. _____

D. As you prepare for the debate, you can predict that the other side will use procedural statements and supporting notions of feasibility, plausibility, and credibility that support their side of the argument. You can argue against these statements by pointing out weaknesses in how these ideas could be implemented. To illustrate, the other side may argue that dangers to national security require that a society surrender all personal freedoms. You could argue that such a policy or procedure would lack social support and, thus, lose credibility.

Review the text and list five key procedural statements that the other side could use in their side of the debate. Then list how you would argue against these statements.

1. _____

2. _____

3. _____

4. _____

5. _____

E. Review and application of previous debate strategies:

In Units 1–4, we covered the first four of the five debate strategies: conjecture, definition, cause and effect, and value. In preparation for the debate, apply these strategies to support your argument or weaken the argument of the other side. Plan ways that you can use all these strategies during the debate.

Framing Templates

A. The following expressions can be used to **stand your ground**. Review these framing templates and incorporate them into both your oral and written arguments.

1. Proponents of X are right to argue that. . . . But they exaggerate when they claim that. . . .

2. While it is true that . . . , it does not necessarily follow that. . . .

3. On the one hand, I agree with X that. . . .

4. But on the other hand, I still insist that. . . .

5. While it seems reasonable that . . . , I would still like to object on the grounds that. . . .

Dealing with Questions

A. There may be times during the debate when you need to **express opinions versus addressing facts**. Use the following statements in case this situation arises.
- I am afraid I cannot provide you with empirical evidence right now, but if you are interested in my opinion, I would say. . . .
- I could cite specific facts, but in my opinion, ...
- I am afraid I cannot cite the particular source, but I once heard somebody say ". . . ," and I agree entirely.

Speaking

A. **Oral Presentation:** Prepare a three- to five-minute oral presentation arguing your position. After practicing, record your presentation and then listen to it. What areas do you need to improve on? Be prepared to give your presentation in class.

B. **Debate:** Now it's time for you to debate. Synthesize all your notes dealing with arguments, useful active vocabulary collocations, and framing templates to assist you during the actual debate. Remember that these will serve as a reference only, not as a text to be read directly during your debate.

Reflection

Self-Evaluation
Think back over the work you have done thus far. Plot your responses to the following statements on the scale.

1. I felt prepared to debate this topic.
2. I was motivated to debate this topic.
3. I put a lot of effort into preparing to debate this topic.

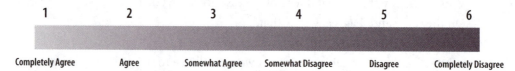

1	2	3	4	5	6
Completely Agree	Agree	Somewhat Agree	Somewhat Disagree	Disagree	Completely Disagree

B. If most of your answers were at the right end of the spectrum, what can you do to move to the left end? If most of your answers were at the left end of the spectrum, what can you do to stay in that area?

Vocabulary Recall

Identify **ten** active vocabulary collocations you have learned and used in this chapter that you feel were most beneficial to you as you debated.

1. _____
2. _____
3. _____
4. _____
5. _____
6. _____
7. _____
8. _____
9. _____
10. _____

UNIT
6

Education versus Field Experience

Academic Qualification: Passport to Success?

Pre-Reading

Introducing the Issue

A. Outside of class, interview nonnative and (if possible) native English speakers that you believe have successful careers. Record their answers to the questions below.
1. How would you define a successful career?
2. What qualifications does a person need in order to start a successful career?
3. What advice would you give to young people entering the workforce?

B. Use the internet to search for three jobs you would like to have. Write a few of the qualifications listed for each job. Are these requirements similar to those you listed in the second question above?

C. Now, get into groups and present the results of your survey to a few of your class-mates. Make sure to answer the questions below and also create two questions of your own to generate a group discussion.
1. Did you find that most people had a similar definition of a successful career?
2. What might account for the variance or similarity in responses to the last two survey questions?
3. According to your quick online job search, what advice do you feel is most helpful to those pursuing a successful career?

4. _____

5. _____

D. Study **Language Note 1** on the meaning of "success" from the *Collins Cobuild Dictionary* and explain how these definitions correlate with those you collected through your survey at the beginning of this unit.

Language Note 1
Success (NOUN)

1. The achievement of something that you have been trying to do.	*Example*: The long-term success of any diet depends on a variety of food choices.
2. The achievement of a high position in a particular field, such as business or politics.	*Example*: Nearly all of the young people interviewed believed that work was the key to success.
3. The fact that something works in a satisfactory way or has the intended result.	*Example*: Enthused by the success of the first exhibition, its organizers are hoping to repeat the experience.
4. Someone or something that achieves a high position, earns a lot of money, or is greatly admired.	*Example*: The project was a great success.

E. Study **Cultural Note 1** and analyze the title "Academic Qualification: Passport to Success?" Make a list of possible issues that could appear in the article.

Cultural Note 1   The Ivy League is composed of eight private universities in the northeastern United States that are known for their academic excellence, selectivity in admissions, and social elitism. These schools often are ranked among the best in the world and, therefore, attract some of the finest and brightest. It is widely believed that degrees from Princeton or Yale are likely to ensure a successful future. Interestingly, though, a number of Ivy League dropouts, such as Matt Damon, Mark Zuckerberg, and Bill Gates, have become rich and famous in spite of abandoning prestigious degrees in pursuit of other dreams.

1. _____

2. _____

3. _____

4. _____

5. _____

Creating Mind Maps

A. Brainstorm as many words as you know associated with personal and academic success. Arrange your ideas to create two separate mind maps according to the pattern shown below. After reading the article, you will be able to add more information so leaving boxes blank at this point is okay.

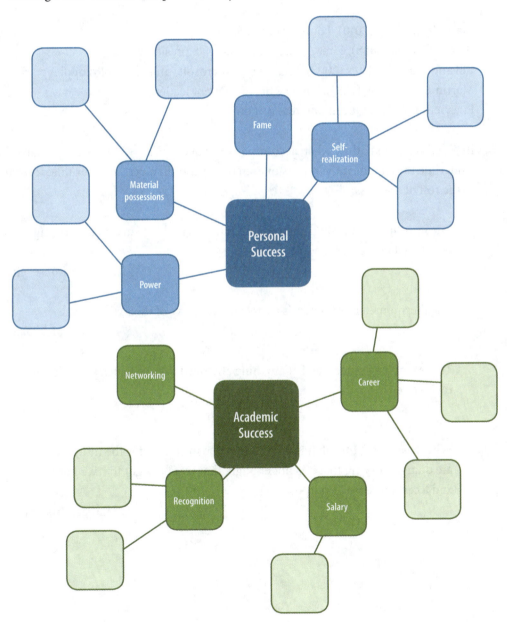

B. Compare your maps with those of your classmates to generate additional ideas. After completing each of the two maps, decide which topic areas can help bridge the gap between the two maps. In other words, which issues concerning personal and academic success intersect?

Discussing Facts and Opinions

A. *Time* magazine identified the following individuals as Persons of the Year. Discuss with a partner what "success" likely meant for each of these distinguished people.

Mark Zuckerberg (2010): Founder of Facebook
Barack Obama (2008): First African American US president
Bill and Melinda Gates (2005): Founder of Microsoft, philanthropic couple
Martin Luther King (1963): Civil rights movement leader
Elizabeth II (1952): Queen of Great Britain

B. If "A + B = Success," then what, according to the quotes below, are the key variables? Underline the significant variables in each quote and then present your final formula to the rest of the class.

> The most important single ingredient in the formula of success is knowing how to get along with people.
>
>   Theodore Roosevelt

> The thermometer of success is merely the jealousy of the malcontents.
>
>   Salvador Dali

> Those who have succeeded at anything and don't mention luck are kidding themselves.
>
>   Larry King

> What is success? I think it is a mixture of having a flair for the thing that you are doing; knowing that it is not enough, that you have got to have hard work and a certain sense of purpose.
>
>   Margaret Thatcher

Success consists of going from failure to failure without loss of enthusiasm.

Winston Churchill

Success is a lousy teacher. It seduces smart people into thinking they can't lose.

Bill Gates

Try not to become a man of success but a man of value.

Albert Einstein

Studying the Topic

Focused Reading

A. As you read "Academic Qualification: Passport to Success?," list the arguments for both sides of the debate in the following table.

Academic Qualification	Field Experience
•	•
•	•
•	•
•	•
•	•
•	•
•	

B. Check your pronunciation of unfamiliar words from the text as you listen to Audio Recording 6.1.

Academic Qualification: Passport to Success?

Brooke Ward

In the sixty years since the United Nations Educational, Scientific and Cultural Organization (UNESCO) set its sights on eradicating illiteracy, significant progress has been made. In the world's most populous areas, an 11 percent increase in overall literacy has been recorded in the last decade alone, with countries like Brazil, China, and Mexico achieving a literacy rate of close to nine out of ten citizens.[1]

Globally, however, one in five adults are still unable to read and write. And, less than 7 percent of today's global population holds a university degree, with a proportional majority of those who do residing in the developed world. For example, university graduates make up well under 1 percent of the population in several African countries, while at the other end of the spectrum, about half of all young Canadians and Russians have received advanced degrees.

While literacy and academic qualification are not one and the same, the former is requisite for the latter, and both have been observed to impact a myriad of other social factors, including gender and ethnic equality, health, political participation, and even economic growth. Given the link to such development issues, many governments and nonprofit organizations see education of the broader population as an agent of progress. Finding a way to educate the masses would ensure individual success, elevate families, and improve entire nations.[2]

Around the world, gaining access to education represents one of the greatest barriers to financial success, and it doesn't just affect the underprivileged. In many countries, students must compete for admission even to lower-ranking institutions. As of 2010 India's higher education system could only accommodate 12 percent of the country's college-age population.[3]

Even if one successfully gains access to higher education, financing it often presents an insurmountable obstacle. In countries such as Sweden, where tuition is free, a number of other significant costs arise, including books, living expenses, and, in the short term, loss of income. Scholarships, grants, and loan programs offer some reprieve but cannot bridge the gap for all students. Student debt is increasing worldwide, even as countries like New Zealand and South Africa attempt to soften the postgraduation blow by making repayment plans dependent on earnings.

Community colleges and similar institutions have increased accessibility and affordability of higher education but also have contributed to a more stratified hierarchy of higher education systems. In North America especially, such institutions are often seen as merely a stepping-stone to other colleges and universities. Even so, research indicates that the likelihood of a community college student continuing on to a four-year degree program is largely a function of his or her family's socioeconomic status, regardless of race or ethnicity.[4]

The wealth of a given nation, and even of each university within that nation, is a key factor in the overall quality of the academic qualification it provides. As such, developing nations are at a significant disadvantage. In Africa, for example, universities struggle to find a place in world institutional rankings and produce a minute fraction of the world's research output. With millions of students electing to study outside of their home country every year, such countries experience a net outward flow of students, particularly those of affluence. The most damaging part of this trend is that many who leave to study abroad often do not return. For example, more than 30 percent of highly educated Ghanaians and Sierra Leoneans live abroad, creating a brain drain where it can ill be afforded.[5]

With such a small percentage of the world's population possessing academic qualification and an abundance of examples of those who find outrageous success without a string of alphabet soup behind their name, a debate over the necessity of higher education emerges. Does academic qualification really ensure success in life?

Before considering the arguments, it is imperative to consider the notion of success. Defined broadly, success is a favorable outcome for a given desire or endeavor. As such, it is highly subjective, a sort of "in the eye of the beholder" scenario. What one person views as a successful outcome—say, a happy marriage

and healthy children—may be viewed by another as a dismal failure because it does not include wealth, power, or fame.

No matter how one defines success, proponents of academic qualification suggest that higher education improves the chances of obtaining it. They point to studies indicating that those who are highly educated tend to have healthier behaviors and fewer instances of single parenthood, for example. However, the strongest arguments revolve around the interpretation of success as accumulation of wealth or prestige.

Knowledge is power, and achieving academic qualification is like building a foundation on rock, they say. This argument is used particularly in the developed world, where career advancement and even getting one's foot in the door depends on academic qualification. While the field of study may be more or less important, depending on the job, a university education provides basic transferable skills, including research and writing skills, interpersonal communication, time management, and other desirable characteristics that are applicable in all disciplines.

Those with higher academic qualification also tend to have secure jobs that are less susceptible to market fluctuations and enjoy a much lower rate of unemployment. Such qualification also offers greater opportunities for social mobility, as evidenced in today's knowledge economy. Oprah Winfrey was born to a poverty-stricken single teen mom in Mississippi, but she was a strong student who earned a full scholarship to Tennessee

State University. Using her education in communications and her own innovatively intimate approach to daytime talk shows, Oprah catapulted herself to a household name, becoming the first black woman billionaire in the world.[6]

Oprah may be an exceptional example, but research has proven that lifetime income is higher for university graduates. Depending on the competitiveness of the institution, such individuals can expect to earn between a quarter and a half a million more over their working lifetime, and that figure increases with further qualification.[7] A full 7 percent of the world's five hundred richest people have PhDs or professional degrees. A further 18 percent have graduate degrees. A total of 60 percent have at least an undergraduate degree, and almost without exception, all have high school diplomas.[8] That's already a significantly higher proportion than the general population of the world at all education levels, but it's interesting to note that almost half of the fabulously wealthy who do not have degrees were heirs to their fortunes. Another fourth of those without degrees established their businesses and organizations in a radically different social and economic climate between 1930 and 1960. Several without degrees were also university dropouts, most often from such institutions as Harvard, which requires a certain level of academic achievement for admission in the first place. Advocates of higher education would take this example to signify that even without achieving a degree, those who spend some time at a university benefit from networking with well-connected professors, faculty, and peers, and from exposure to new ideas and perceptions.

On the flip side, there are those who argue that education is irrelevant because success is a product of hard work, natural talent, people skills, and, frequently, good luck (some say fate). Millions of young people around the world will never have an opportunity to obtain academic qualification, they point out, but some of them will be successful beyond their wildest dreams because of factors beyond their control.

There is also a prevailing undercurrent in America suggesting that upward mobility is available irrespective of education. This is reflected most pointedly in celebrity culture, from movie stars to star athletes and internet pundits and politicians, where fame and fortune often go hand in hand.

In an episode of the popular American adult cartoon series *The Simpsons*, the twenty-something founder of Facebook, Mark Zuckerberg, uses the example of fellow self-made billionaires Bill Gates (Microsoft) and Richard Branson (Virgin Group) as examples when he tells young Lisa that she does not need to graduate from college to be incredibly successful, never mind that both Zuckerberg and Gates are dropouts of one of the most prestigious universities in the world (Harvard).[9] Examples of very wealthy people who never earned university degrees abound, especially in the domains of sports and entertainment. Elite athletes and movie stars are among the best-paid professionals in the world, often raking in eight-figure salaries. Even the least experienced rookies in the major leagues stand to make more in a year than the average American, not to mention individuals from other nations, will make over the course of his lifetime.

"Formal education stifles creativity and causes masses to think alike," is another argument of some who advocate against the need for academic qualification. Academic qualification didn't prevent countless people from losing their jobs in the financial crisis of 2007–8, and many university graduates, even from the most prestigious schools, do not achieve great financial success. Education also does not ensure against serious crime, they point out. In Asia, one in five convicted sex offenders has at least a bachelor's degree.[10]

What's more, academic qualification rarely has any relevance to jobs that graduates are employed to do, and in a hurting global economy, that translates into a mass of overqualified people with advanced degrees who are less willing to do the menial jobs that exist. Besides, there are other factors that are better determinants of success, including satisfaction with life and personal relationships.

For Americans, the concept of success is deeply rooted in financial prosperity and is traditionally linked to some form of education. The first university established in the United States was Harvard in 1636, and the federal government began to support institutions of higher learning by the end of the 1800s. Thomas Jefferson was an early proponent of financial aid, believing that talented and hardworking students without financial means still deserved to attend a university and reap the benefits.[11]

The twentieth century was a time of educational revolution worldwide, but this was particularly evident in the United States, with enrollment jumping from just 2 percent of the college-age population at the beginning of the century to over half of Americans of the same demographic today. Enrollment soared after World War II, when returned servicemen saw education as an opportunity to gain a competitive advantage.

The United States was the first country to achieve mass higher education, and it is among the leaders in female education rates. A total of 87 percent of adult US citizens have graduated from high school, over half have completed some college, and 38 percent have an associate or bachelor's degree.[12] Advanced degrees are still possessed by a very small percentage of the population, but academic trends indicate that a larger number of young Americans are earning advanced degrees and as a group are becoming more qualified academically than previous generations. Today women in America already make up the majority of those earning advanced degrees.[13]

While it is generally accepted that academic qualification does not guarantee success, Americans, along with many other cultures, generally recognize that it is an asset. "What do you do?" is one of the first questions asked in many societies, and the answer to that question can usually provide some insight into how much schooling an individual has. Whether admitted or not, individual academic qualification has a significant impact on social interactions such as friendship circles and marriage candidacy, both in the developed and developing worlds.

Governments and nonprofit organizations worldwide continue to push to improve access and quality of education based on the assumption that higher education provides more opportunities in life. Are they correct in this assumption, or are there other factors that are better predictors of success? And as younger generations in the developed world increasingly become more educated than their parents, does that dilute the value of a higher education or does that make it more important to obtain one?

Notes

1. R. Car-Hill, *International Literacy Statistics: A Review of Concepts, Methodology and Current Data* (Montreal: UNESCO Institute for Statistics, 2008).
2. P. G. Altbach, L. Reisberg, and L. E. Rumbley, *Trends in Global Higher Education: Tracking an Academic Revolution* (Paris: UNESCO World Conference on Higher Education, 2009).
3. K. Fisher, "In India, a Student-Recruiting Industry Ups the Ante for US Colleges," *Chronicle of Higher Education*, January 10, 2010, http://chronicle.com/article/In-India-a-Student -Recruiting/63467/.
4. US Department of Education—Institute of Education Sciences, *Digest of Education Statistics* (Washington: National Center for Education Statistics, 2010).
5. "Education at a Glance 2009," Organisation for Economic Co-Operation and Development, modified September 2009, www .oecd.org/education/skills-beyond-school /educationataglance2009oecdindicators.htm.
6. "Oprah Winfrey," Biography.com, accessed October 22, 2013, www.biography.com/people /oprah-winfrey-9534419.
7. J. Klor de Alva and M. Schneider, *Who Wins? Who Pays? The Economic Returns and Costs of a Bachelor's Degree* (Washington, DC: American Institutes for Research, 2011).
8. "The World's Billionaires," *Forbes*, modified or March 14, 2013, www.forbes.com/wealth /billionaires.
9. "Mark Zuckerberg," Biography.com, accessed October 22, 2013, www.biography.com/people /mark-zuckerberg-507402?page=1.
10. "One in Five Sex Criminals University Grads: Survey," *Korea Herald*, Asia News Network, March 16, 2010, http://news.asiaone.com/News /Education/Story/A1Story20100315-204755 .html.
11. "Early History of Universities in America," *Education History*, accessed October 22, 2013, www.ajha.org/early-history-of-universities-in -america.htm.
12. "Educational Attainment in the United States: 2009," US Census Bureau, modified September 22, 2010, www.census.gov/hhes/socdemo /education/data/cps/2009/tables.html.
13. "EFA Global Monitoring Report," UNESCO, accessed October 22, 2013, www.unesco .org/new/en/education/themes/leading-the -international-agenda/efareport/.

Checking Comprehension

A. Based on the text, indicate whether each statement is true or false. Modify false statements to make them true.

1. In the world's most populous areas, an insignificant increase in overall literacy has been recorded in the last decade.

2. Literacy guarantees academic success regardless of a nation's economic development.

3. Both literacy and academic qualification have been linked to an improvement in gender, ethnic, health, political, and economic issues.

4. Assistance in the form of scholarships, grants, and loans helps offset the cost of education for some students.

5. An African American college student is less likely than a white (American) college student of the same socioeconomic status to pursue a four-year degree after studying at a community college.

6. According to the article, studying outside one's own country might negatively impact the home country in terms of possible brain drain.

7. Evidence in the article suggests that it is not possible to become wealthy without at least some academic experience at or beyond high school graduation.

8. For Americans, the concept of success is not traditionally associated with academic achievement.

9. Proponents of academic qualification admit that, depending on one's definition of success, education may or may not improve the likelihood of having a successful future.

10. Although the United States was the first country to bring higher education to the masses, advanced degrees are still possessed by only a small percentage of the population.

Mastering Vocabulary

Active Vocabulary Collocations	
Education and Success	**General**
1. academic qualification/achievement	1. beyond one's control
2. well-paid workers	2. beyond one's wildest dreams
3. determinants of success	3. favorable outcome
4. financial aid	4. in the first place
5. financial success/prosperity	5. nonprofit organizations
6. heir to a fortune	6. at one end of the spectrum
7. high school diploma	7. on the flip side
8. low/high-ranking institutions	8. to be based on the assumption
9. prestigious schools	9. to be deeply rooted in
10. to compete for admission	10. to be traditionally linked to
11. to ensure individual success	11. to dilute the value of
12. to graduate from college/a university	12. to have a competitive advantage
13. to earn, receive, hold a degree	13. to go hand in hand
14. undergraduate/graduate/postgraduate degrees	14. to make progress
15. university/college dropout	15. to reap the benefits

Expanding Vocabulary

A. Complete the mind maps begun in the pre-reading section by using active vocabulary collocations. In order to do this, you may need to expand your mind maps by adding new boxes and connections.

B. ⊕ Go to COCA (http://corpus.byu.edu/coca/). Click on COLLOCATES, and type "[v*]" in the box that appears. Under SORTING AND LIMITS find the dropdown menu next to MINIMUM and select MUTUAL INFO. For each word below, type each collocation in the WORD(S) box and click SEARCH. Write three collocates commonly used in conjunction with each word in the left-hand column.

Education & Success	Corresponding Collocates		
1. Diploma	a. earn	b. receive	c. obtain
2. Assumption			
3. Benefits			
4. Success			
5. Control			
6. Advantage			
7. Admission			
8. Dropout			
9. Progress			
10. Value			

C. Choose five collocations concerning education and success from the previous activity. Write a sentence for each collocation that either supports or condemns entering the workforce immediately instead of pursuing an advanced degree.

1. _____

2. _____

3. _____

4. _____

5. _____

D. Fill in the blanks with the collocations from the Word Bank.

Word Bank		
well-paid workers	reap the benefits	academic qualification
financial aid	high school diploma	high-ranking institution
goes hand in hand	beyond one's control	to earn an undergradu-
competing for admission	prestigious schools	ate degree
heir to a fortune	based on the assumption	

During their last year of high school, students face an important decision regarding their future. Some believe that a (1) _____ is not enough to ensure a successful career. This thinking is (2) _____ that most (3) _____ landed their jobs because they possessed both experience and (4) _____. Thus, these students apply to (5) _____ in order (6) _____. However, the majority of (7) _____ are expensive and, in most cases, applicants rely on (8) _____ since not everyone can boast of being an (9) _____. At the same time, there are those who are convinced that success (10) _____ with luck. They are sure that one's fate is (11) _____ and that there's no use in (12) _____ with someone luckier, richer, and smarter. Instead, they prefer to enter the workforce straight out of high school and expect to (13) _____ of their skills and talents rather than from academic achievements.

Exploring the Meaning

A. Write out as many active vocabulary collocations as possible that can be used in a cover letter for a university or job application. Some collocations may fall into several categories.

Applying to a University	Applying for a Job
•	•
•	•
•	•
•	•
•	•
•	•

B. With a partner, role-play an interview either with a college admissions officer or a human resources officer using the active vocabulary collocations from one of the columns above. Take turns being the interviewer and the interviewee.

C. Paraphrase the sentences below using the active vocabulary collocations in brackets.
   1. I couldn't ever have imagined that I would achieve so much. [beyond one's wildest dreams]
   2. Your grammar has improved since you started writing more. [to make progress]
   3. Instead of finishing his college studies, the young man decided to devote his life to art. [college dropout]
   4. A desire to do well in school usually is associated with aspirations for a higher social status. [to be traditionally linked to]
   5. According to the Protestant work ethic, spiritual wealth and material wealth go hand in hand. [financial prosperity]

6. Success stories of people who never went to school can diminish the importance of education in modern society. [to dilute the value of]

7. His PhD gave him an edge over other applicants competing for an assistant professor position. [to have a competitive advantage]

8. Few believed that the project would be successful. [favorable outcome]

9. Starting a family right out of high school resulted in the young woman delaying a college education. [on the flip side]

10. The race for success stems from the American dream. [to be deeply rooted in]

Discussing the Article

A. Working with a partner, use active vocabulary collocations to answer the following questions based on the text.

1. Why is educating as many members of society as possible in a country's best interest?

2. What is the link between literacy and academic qualification?

3. Assuming that students always have been responsible for costs such as books and living expenses, why is student debt increasing worldwide?

4. Why are developing nations at a disadvantage in terms of the academic qualification they provide?

5. What is "brain drain?" How can developing nations avoid it?

6. Are there objective ways to define "success?" If yes, what are they? If no, why not? Should success be defined by the "accumulation of wealth and/or prestige?" Why or why not?

7. Are people more likely to be "successful" with or without an education?

8. In what ways is knowledge power? In what ways is it not? What is more important in the job market: academic qualification or field experience?

9. What factors contribute to one's ability to pursue higher education? What factors contribute to one's ability to become successful? Why do certain people enjoy more financial success than others?

10. Are there too many overqualified people in the workforce? Would the workforce benefit from more or fewer educated individuals? Support your opinion.

Constructing Critical Discourse

Recognizing Logical Fallacies

A. In Unit 5 we discussed five logical fallacies that might occur in argumentation during debates. Here we will learn about five more equally weak argumentative techniques and their distinguishing features.

Explanation	Example
Straw Man	
Misrepresenting or overstating an opponent's position so as to attack or refute him/her.	*Creationists do not believe that animals change, but clearly they do change. So, creationists are wrong.*
Appeal to Emotion	
Manipulating emotions rather than using valid logic to win an argument	*You can't fail me because my parents will be very angry.*
Begging the Question	
Stating that something is true though it has yet to be proven so	*I know God exists because it's written in the Bible, and I know the Bible is true because it was written by God.*
Either / Or	
Making broad statements that something is true/right based on insufficient or limited evidence	*I saw two white squirrels in New York. All squirrels in New York are white.*
Faulty Cause / Effect	
Falsely assuming that one event caused the next	*The more firemen fighting a fire the larger the fire. Firemen only make fires worse.*

B. Now read the following statements and decide if they are logically sound or faulty.
If you discover a logical fallacy, identify what type it is.

1. Professors want you to believe you will never be a success unless you have a PhD,
   but I'm here to tell you they're wrong.
2. Over the years more and more women have been seeking higher education, and
   simultaneously the economy has declined. Educating women is leading to the
   downfall of our nation and should be stopped.
3. Statistics show that those who receive a higher education generally earn more
   money than those who don't.
4. To become rich and famous, you either have to drop out of college early or have
   connections in the workforce.
5. If you have friends in high places, you scarcely need an education to get a job.
   So it's often not what you know but who you know that matters most.
6. I work hard every single day to pay for your tuition and give you opportunities I
   never had. If you don't go to college you will break my heart.
7. With so many people today getting college degrees, there are fewer individuals
   willing to do menial tasks, such as cleaning or landscaping.
8. Dan can tell you what a good employee I am and why I deserve a raise. If you
   don't trust Dan, I can certainly vouch for his character.

Forming Hypotheses

A. Study the following abstract from "Utopia," by Sir Thomas More and published in
1516. In his discussion of a perfect society, what does the author propose as a model
for an ideal education?

> There are but few in any town that are so wholly excused from labor as to give
> themselves entirely up to their studies, these being only such persons as dis-
> cover from their childhood an extraordinary capacity and disposition for let-
> ters; yet their children, and a great part of the nation, both men and women,
> are taught to spend those hours in which they are not obliged to work in read-
> ing: and this they do through the whole progress of life. They have all their
> learning in their own tongue, which is both a copious and pleasant language,
> and in which a man can fully express his mind. It is ordinary to have public
> lectures every morning before daybreak, at which none are obliged to appear
> but those who are marked out for literature; yet a great many, both men and
> women of all ranks, go to hear lectures of one sort or other, according to their
> inclinations.

B. Using the pattern shown below for constructing hypotheses, respond, based on More's vision of education, to the following questions regarding education.

Conditions in the past, present, or future	+	Implications for the past, present, or future
• If something **had happened** then,		• something else **would have been** different then.
• If something **happened** now, →		• something else **would happen** now.
• If something **happens** in the future,		• something else **will happen** in the future.

1. What changes might have come about in world history if More's model had been implemented starting in 1516? What would the world look like now if More's ideas had been adopted?
2. What would happen if a society tried to enforce More's vision of education now?
3. If More's ideas ever come about, what will be the effect on countries in particular, and the global community in general (especially taking into consideration More's comment about education in one's "own tongue")?

Practice Debate

A. Choose one of the roles below and role-play it using at least ten active vocabulary collocations per person.

Situation: The City Council is holding a meeting with representatives from the community to discuss the creation of a nonprofit organization to raise scholarship money to sponsor gifted students (regardless of financial need) and to help them succeed in the future.

Role A: A wealthy representative who believes that academic credentials do not play a crucial role in determining future success and, therefore, is opposed to creating a community scholarship fund.

Role B: A well-off representative who, despite his family wealth, believes that success comes to those who work hard. Accordingly, he favors the idea of creating a community scholarship fund.

Role C: A middle-income representative who believes that all people should have a chance to receive a college education and, thus, supports creating a community scholarship fund.

Role D: A low-income representative who believes that a community scholarship fund is incapable of raising anyone from poverty and that the destiny of the poor is to make a living by working hard, not wasting time on education.

Listening

Pre-Listening

A. Before listening to the audio file, predict the arguments that you'll hear. Fill in the table below.

Academic qualification ensures success in life.	Field experience ensures success in life.
•	•
•	•
•	•
•	•
•	•
•	•
•	•

While Listening

A. **Listening for general comprehension:** Listen to Audio Recording 6.2 and put a check next to arguments that appear in the table. Write down additional arguments that initially were missing in your table.

B. **Listening for specific details:** Listen to the audio file a second time and evaluate the arguments you listed in the table above as "strong" or "weak." Propose ways of improving the arguments you labeled as "weak."

Post-Listening

A. Which side do you think presented a more persuasive argument? Support your opinion by citing their strongest argument.

B. In every debate, someone has the last word. Predict what the opposing side's response would be to the final argument you heard.

Formatting the Argument: Writing

Write Your Own Position Paper

A. Write a position paper regarding the education versus field experience debate. Then, observe the following guidelines for revising your essay.

Revising Essays

1. Consider the content and organization of the essay before correcting the language and sentence structure.
2. Be open to the possibility that your final draft may differ significantly from your initial version. Revision often means throwing out ideas that aren't relevant or reworking ideas that aren't fully developed.
3. Underline your topic sentences in each paragraph. If a topic sentence is missing, draft one.
4. Highlight your thesis statement in the introduction and your rephrased thesis statement in the conclusion. Reread the topic sentences you previously underlined and make sure that they support your thesis.
5. Consider the order in which your paragraphs appear. Check the logic behind the organization of your paper and the sequencing of ideas.
6. Ensure that evidence fits your claims. Without data, your claims are merely statements of opinion.
7. Make sure that your essay effectively deals with a significant counterargument. If it does not address a counterargument, you may lose credibility with your reader.
8. Proofread your paper for grammar and vocabulary mistakes.

A. Read the following essay and evaluate it using the steps above. What improvements could be made to the essay?

Education versus Field Experience: Position Paper

With worldwide economic problems and the seemingly ever-increasing cost of higher education, many prospective students wonder if academic qualifications are worth the cost. Paying for tuition for four years is projected to cost $127,100 at a private university and $37,800 for an in-state resident at a public university.[1] *USA Today* reported that from 2008 to 2010, the average tuition at a four-year university climbed 15 percent.[2] However, even though the cost of higher education is rising, the potential benefits of academic qualifications are undeniable because they improve the chances of achieving success.

Studies have shown that those who achieve higher academic qualifications are more employable and have a higher earning potential than those who have less education. For example, one study showed that on average, a person with less than a high school diploma makes $451 a week, while someone with a high school diploma makes $638. A person with an associate's degree makes an average of $768 a week, but a person with a bachelor's degree brings home an average of $1,053 weekly. Getting a postgraduate degree further increases a person's average earnings. Similarly, this same study showed that while those with less than a high school diploma suffered from a 14.1 percent unemployment rate, people with some college had only an 8.7 percent rate, and people with a professional or doctoral degree had only a 2.4 percent rate of unemployment.[3]

Some studies have shown that those with a college education have happier marriages than those without.[4] A number of studies also show a correlation between higher education and increased awareness of a healthy lifestyle, for example, more time spent at the gym and healthier eating habits.[5] A college education also tends to provide greater opportunities for promotion and upward social mobility.[6] Nationwide, only 18 percent of the general population eighteen years of age or older has not completed high school, but about 41 percent of inmates in state and federal prisons and jails have not completed high school or its equivalent.[7]

Some of the top earners in the world either did not attend college or dropped out before receiving their degree. Among the most famous college dropouts are Steve Jobs, founder and former CEO of Apple; Bill Gates, founder and former CEO of Microsoft; and Mark Zuckerburg, founder and CEO of Facebook. Moreover, some jobs that require no education pay more than jobs requiring high levels of education. For example, as of 2008, most experienced national sales representatives who close big deals (between $200,000 and $2,000,000) earn $110,000 a year in salary and bonuses. That salary is higher than the salaries of 95 percent of tenured professors of English, a job that requires a PhD.[8]

Evidence shows that a person with a college degree, regardless of what field the degree is in, will be more likely to avoid unemployment, achieve a higher income, and remain healthier and happier than a person without a college degree. They are also more likely to show tolerance toward others of differing beliefs. Even though higher education is expensive, the benefits of obtaining academic qualifications are undeniable.

Notes

1. "The Real Cost of Higher Education," *Saving-forcollege.com*, accessed October 22, 2013, www .savingforcollege.com/tutorial101/the_real_cost _of_higher_education.php.

2. Christine Armario, "Average Cost of Four-Year University Up 15%," *USA Today*, June 13, 2012, http://usatoday30.usatoday.com/money /economy/story/2012-06-13/college-costs-surge /55568278/1.

3. "Employment Projections: Education Pays," *Bureau of Labor Statistics*, March 23, 2012, www .bls.gov/emp/ep_chart_001.htm.

4. Institute for American Values, University of Virginia, *The State of Our Unions: Marriage in America 2012* (Charlottesville, VA: National Marriage Project, 2012), www.stateofourunions .org/2012/SOOU2012.pdf.

5. "College Degree Linked with Better Health, Study Finds," *Huffington Post*, March 1, 2012, www.huffingtonpost.com/2012/03/01/college -degree-health-graduate-20s-midlife_n _1311006.html.

6. Lisa Smith, "Invest in Yourself with a College Education," *Investopedia*, March 25, 2012, www .investopedia.com/articles/younginvestors/06 /investineducation.asp#axzz2GgGLBtj9.

7. Caroline Wolf Harlow, "Education and Correctional Populations," *US Department of Justice*, modified April 15, 2003, http://bjs.ojp.usdoj.gov /content/pub/pdf/ecp.pdf.

8. Rachel Zupek, "Does Your Major Limit Your Earning Power?," *Career Builder*, February 27, 2009, www.careerbuilder.com/Article/CB-663 -Job-Search-Does-Your-Major-Limit-Your -Earning-Power/.

B. Exchange essays with a classmate. Use the preceding guidelines to peer review each other's papers. Explain the rationale for your suggestions. Revise your essay based on comments received.

Formatting the Argument: Speaking

Implementing Rhetorical Strategies

A. Study the following note:

> **Strategy Note 1**   In this last unit, we will apply the five rhetorical strategies covered in the previous chapters to this topic. Remember that these strategies are:
>
> 1. Conjecture (What if . . . ?) questions: What would happen if everyone received high academic qualification?
> 2. Definition questions: What does it mean to be educated?
> 3. Cause and effect questions: What are the likely results of large numbers of poor people not receiving a reasonable formal education?

    4. Value questions: Does government have a moral responsibility to provide high-quality, advanced education to everyone?

    5. Procedural questions: Considering rising costs, how can we make advanced education more accessible?

B. Review the text highlighting important words or phrases that you could use to support your side of the debate. For example, if you are arguing that hard work rather than education is key to success, look for words and phrases that may be used to support your case, regardless of which strategy you employ.

C. Provide examples of each of the five debate strategies covered in Units 1–5. When debating, apply these strategies to support your argument or weaken the argument of the other side.

    1. Conjecture

    2. Definition

    3. Cause and effect

    4. Value

    5. Procedure

D. As you prepare for the debate, you can predict that the other side will use statements that support their side of the argument. You can argue against these statements by pointing out weaknesses in how these ideas could be implemented.

    Review the text and list five key points that the other side could use in their side of the debate. Then list how you would argue against these relationships. Try to apply all five rhetorical strategies in responding to these arguments.

    1. _____

    2. _____

    3. _____

    4. _____

    5. _____

Framing Templates

A. The following expressions can be used to **reach a compromise**. Review these framing templates and incorporate them into both your oral and written arguments.

1. When it comes to X, most of us will readily agree that . . .
2. While X is probably wrong to claim that . . . , it is right to say that . . .
3. I do support X's position on . . . , but I also find Y's argument about . . . equally persuasive.
4. Both X and Y have strong arguments in favor and against . . . , but I would probably side with . . .
5. We should admit that X is right to believe that . . . ; however Y also raised valid reasons for . . .

Dealing with Questions

A. There may be times during the debate when you **are unable to answer a question**. Use the following statements in case this situation arises.

- Unfortunately, I am unable to answer this question.
- I apologize but I would prefer not to answer simply because . . .
- I am afraid I will not be able to answer your question because . . .
- Although this issue deserves further discussion, I do not think I can provide a good answer right now.

Speaking

A. Oral Presentation: Prepare a three- to five-minute oral presentation arguing your position. After practicing, record your presentation and then listen to it. What areas do you need to improve on? Be prepared to give your presentation in class.

B. Debate: Now it's time for you to debate. Synthesize all your notes dealing with arguments, useful active vocabulary collocations, and framing templates to assist you during the actual debate. Remember that these will serve as a reference only, not as a text to be read directly during your debate.

Reflection

Self-Evaluation

A. Think back over the work you have done thus far. Plot your responses to the following statements on the scale.
1. I felt prepared to debate this topic.
2. I was motivated to debate this topic.
3. I put a lot of effort into preparing to debate this topic.

1	2	3	4	5	6
Completely Agree	Agree	Somewhat Agree	Somewhat Disagree	Disagree	Completely Disagree

B. If most of your answers were at the right end of the spectrum, what can you do to move to the left end? If most of your answers were at the left end of the spectrum, what can you do to stay in that area?

Vocabulary Recall

Identify **ten** active vocabulary collocations you have learned and used in this chapter that you feel were most beneficial to you as you debated.

1. _____
2. _____
3. _____
4. _____
5. _____
6. _____
7. _____
8. _____
9. _____
10. _____

Appendix A

STRUCTURING A DEBATE

Rationale

A number of different debate formats could be applied to the topics presented in this textbook. However, given that Parliamentary Debate, or region-specific versions of it, serves as the leading format at the university level, the instructions and methods laid out below reflect the parliamentary style.

Teams and Roles

To organize and run a debate in your classroom, the authors recommend the following protocol:

1. Divide the class into two teams: proposition (those speaking in favor of a motion) and opposition (those against a motion). Traditionally, teams of four compete; however, this number can vary depending on class size.
2. Decide which side of a given debate the proposition and opposition will take.
3. The proposition begins each debate by framing a motion with the wording *This House believes . . .* or *This House would. . . .* For example, if the motion is *This House believes that governments should mandate wealth redistribution*, then the proposition (or "Government") speakers should explain why wealth redistribution is a good idea and the opposition should demonstrate why it is not. Additionally, the government should propose a course of action and support it with philosophical, practical, and consequential arguments. The burden of proof is on the government, but the opposition must also demonstrate the strength of its arguments.[1]
4. Individual speeches alternate between the proposition and opposition and can vary in length, for example, four to seven minutes, depending on class size or experience. Table knocking is perfectly acceptable in parliamentary-style debate and signals to a speaker that team members approve of what is being said.
5. After the first minute and before the last minute of a speech, any member of the opposing team can offer an argument or ask a question, otherwise known as offering "points of information." For example, when any member of the proposition team is speaking, any member of the opposition team can stand for a point of information. In the same way, when any member of the opposition team is speaking, any member of the

---

1. Adapted from "Debate Formats," *IDEA* (International Debate Education Association) January 5, 2013, http://idebate.org/about/debate/formats.

proposition team can stand. Instructors/judges are responsible for keeping time and signaling to debaters when they can offer points of information and when they cannot.

Signals

The authors recommend the following method for signaling debaters when they can and cannot offer points of information and when their time is up.

1. Yellow card: At the start of the first and last minute, the instructor/judge holds up a yellow card to signal to members of the opposing team that they may not offer points of information.
2. Green card: When the first minute is up, the instructor/judge holds up a green card that signals to members of the opposing team that they can offer points of information.
3. Red card: When the final minute has ended, the instructor/judge holds up a red card that signals to the speaker that he or she must stop and sit down.

Assessing Performance

Instructors are encouraged to use the rubric (see appendix B) that reflects a synthesis of criteria developed by the American Council on the Teaching of Foreign Languages.

Appendix B

RUBRIC FOR WRITING AND SPEAKING
(100 POINTS POSSIBLE)

Criteria	Content	Vocabulary	
	Appropriate and complete content, including introduction and conclusion	Accuracy, variety, and appropriateness of word choice	
Fair	**10–13 points** Writer/speaker fails to support his/her claim for various reasons, which may include lack of evidence or analysis for arguments, inability to respond to opposing arguments.	**10–13 points** Vocabulary demonstrates inadequate range and/or inaccuracy. Meaning is confused.	
Good	**14–15 points** Writer/speaker somewhat successfully supports his/her claim. Some evidence or analysis is offered for arguments. Is somewhat able to reply to opposing argument.	**14–15 points** Limited range of vocabulary; use of words is sometimes inaccurate or inappropriate.	
Very Good	**16–17 points** Writer/speaker successfully supports his/her claim. He/she is able to establish a clear position with adequate support. Writer/speaker counters the opposing side's arguments reasonably well.	**16–17 points** Vocabulary is adequate and includes some idiomatic expressions, though writer/speaker may use general terminology rather than specific. Use of words is occasionally inaccurate.	
Excellent	**18–20 points** Writer/speaker makes powerful arguments in support of his/her claim, uses inconsistencies in opposing arguments to his/her advantage, and shows awareness of the complexity of the issue.	**18–20 points** Vocabulary is sophisticated in range and sociolinguistically appropriate.	

Grammar	Structure	Impact
Accuracy, form	**Quantity and organization of language discourse**	**Ability to motivate the audience to continue reading or listening**
10–13 points Major problems in simple and complex constructions; frequent errors of agreement, tense, number, case, etc.	**10–13 points** Variety of complete sentences and cohesive devices. In writing, emerging paragraph-length discourse. Inadequate introduction and/or conclusion.	**10–13 points** Writing or speech lacks fluency; speech is filled with lengthy pauses/writing is disjointed. The audience would quickly become impatient with this essay/speech.
14–15 points Effective but simple constructions, minor problems in complex constructions, several errors of agreement, tense, number, and case.	**14–15 points** Thoughts are logically presented. In writing, complete paragraphs with clear structure and cohesive devices; adequate introduction and conclusion.	**14–15 points** Writing or speech is somewhat choppy. The audience would find the essay/speech difficult to follow.
16–17 points Effective complex constructions, few errors of agreement, tense, number, or case.	**16–17 points** Language moves beyond individual thoughts to a connected whole. In writing, paragraphs are logically structured with adequate introduction and conclusion.	**16–17 points** Writing or speech is smooth and fluid. The audience would find this essay/speech engaging to read/listen to.
18–20 points Virtually no errors.	**18–20 points** Discourse is well organized and structured around a single theme. In writing, effective introduction and conclusion frame logically structured paragraphs in the main body.	**18–20 points** Writing or speech is fluent, with a definite style. The audience would be very motivated to read/listen to this essay/speech.